Uncertain Safari

Kenyan Encounters and African Dreams

Allan M. Winkler

For Cecelia,
With genuine thanks
for making this possible.
With all best wishes,
Allan

Hamilton Books
an imprint of
UNIVERSITY PRESS OF AMERICA,® INC.
Dallas • Lanham • Boulder • New York • Oxford

Copyright © 2004 by
Hamilton Books
4501 Forbes Boulevard
Suite 200
Lanham, Maryland 20706
UPA Acquisitions Department (301) 459-3366

PO Box 317
Oxford
OX2 9RU, UK

Library of Congress Control Number: 2004105231
ISBN 0-7618-2839-7 (clothbound : alk. ppr.)
ISBN 0-7618-2840-0 (paperback : alk. ppr.)

For Sara

Table of Contents

Acknowledgments

I could not have written this book without the help of a number of people in both Kenya and the United States. First of all, I'm grateful to all of those Kenyans who talked to me, whether formally or informally, and helped me understand something about Kenyan society. A number of them became real friends, and need to be singled out. Mary Mwiandi, now finishing her doctorate at Michigan State University, was endlessly patient and generous and really helped me find my way around the University of Nairobi. I'm also grateful to her for letting me write about her own struggle and her eventual triumph. Godfrey and Margaret Muriuki are likewise special friends. When I first arrived in Nairobi, many of the people I met referred me to Godfrey, and once I met him I understood why. He cares genuinely about his students, as well as those not in his classroom, and has the ability to help make the bureaucracy deal appropriately with people who need assistance. His wife Margaret, who ran the University of Nairobi Bookstore until her retirement in 2003, is equally warm and gracious. As I got to know both of them in the year I taught at the University of Nairobi, and on every subsequent visit, I became more and more fond of them, and look forward to seeing them whenever I can. Finally, Gloria Hagberg continues to be a kind of family member — Sara's surrogate mother in Nairobi — and we visit with her regularly whenever we are in Nairobi. I've now known her for more than ten years, and she too is a special friend.

The manuscript is far better thanks to the assistance of a number of people. When I finished a first draft, I asked several friends to read it, and their comments helped me tremendously in the process of revision. Alice Mattison, a wonderful poet and novelist I've know since our infant children began to play together more than thirty years ago, went through the manuscript meticulously, and pointed out the generalities and colloquialisms that were far too common. She also helped me find a voice as I told my story, and I am truly grateful for her advice. Elliott Gorn, who probably writes the best history of any of my professional friends, was likewise critical—and helpful—as he went through the text line by line. I think he hoped I would write a different book, but his suggestions made this one better. Osaak Olumwullah, a Kenyan colleague at Miami University, also read the manuscript very carefully and kept me from making all kinds of errors of fact. I appreciate that critical attention and also the support for pushing ahead. Lawson Wulsin, a fellow academic who likewise worked in Kenya the year I taught at the University of Nairobi, made some very astute comments when he read what I had written about experiences we both shared, and those observations were particularly useful in the rewriting process. Historian Linda K. Kerber and essayist Susan Allen Toth, both writers of note, read the manuscript when it was being considered for publication, and their thoughtful suggestions helped me a great deal in making final revisions. My sister, Karen Winkler Moulton, an editor at the *Chronicle of Higher Education*, has been my own special editor for more than thirty years. She went over my very first book manuscript soon after I completed graduate school, and gave this manuscript the same kind of attention in the midst of an extraordinarily busy work schedule. She deserves an extra special word of thanks. Finally, I want to thank my wife, Sara Penhale, to whom this book is dedicated, for both introducing me to Africa and for sharing the experience on every visit we have made, and for going over the manuscript carefully and making a number of important suggestions as it was ready to go to press.

A Summer Research Appointment and Grant to Promote Research from the Miami University Committee on Faculty Research allowed me to return to Kenya after I had begun to write, and to follow up a number of important issues.

Cecilia Cancellaro believed the book could work, and helped it find a home, and I really appreciate all of her efforts. Nicole Caddigan was willing to take a chance on the manuscript, and I am grateful for that. I would like to thank Jeri Schaner for her secretarial support over a period of years, including sending me necessary materials while I was in East Africa. And I would like to thank Martha Beyerlein, with whom I have worked on a number of books in the past, for her meticulous copyediting at a particularly difficult point in her own life.

This book was one I really wanted to write, as I lived and worked in Africa. I hope I have managed to convey something of the experience, and the affection for a place that has become an important part of my life.

Prologue

In the summer of 1990, I found myself flying across the Sahara, heading for Kenya—and Africa—for the first time. I was excited about visiting a part of the world I had never seen and anxious about what I might find. The British Airways flight from London included black Kenyans going home, white Britons returning to business jobs in Nairobi, and a motley mix of tourists from around the globe. An air of anticipation kept most of us awake as we flew through the night.

Fatigue vanished as we arrived in Nairobi. Exhaustion returned after an interminable delay at the baggage-claim area, when I discovered that one of my bags was missing and I had to file lost-luggage forms with a Kenyan attendant. I could only hope that the next British Airways flight brought the misplaced bag. Despite the assurances of the airline clerk, I was certain I would never see the suitcase again.

At long last, I left the baggage-claim area and entered the main waiting room. American airports often look much the same. Long corridors contain waiting lounges and departure and arrival gates. Muzak seeps out of speakers hidden around every turn, while TV monitors show the latest news from CNN, providing a kind of standardized sterility that makes you forget where you are. Until the terrorist attacks of September 11, 2001, people meeting passengers in the United States could usually go all the way to the arrival area and greet their visitors as they came off the plane.

The Jomo Kenyatta Airport in Kenya was different. All travelers walked into the public waiting area through a single door, spit out like gum balls dropping from a candy machine, one or two at a time. Taxi drivers vied loudly with one another for customers, while tour-company operators held up signs for travelers they were meeting. A blanket of discordant background noise made it hard to get my bearings. The slightly stale smell of sweat, mingled with exhaust fumes, filled the air.

That chaotic first encounter with Africa took me by surprise. I had flown in and out of airports all over Europe and Asia and was usually comfortable finding my way around. Now I began to wonder if I was ready for this excursion to Africa. Was this really where I wanted to be?

In part, my apprehension stemmed from how little I knew about what lay ahead. I had never really thought much about coming to Africa in the past. I had lived in England for a year in the mid-1950s when I was ten and my father had a Fulbright grant to do historical research at the London School of Economics. Memories fade, but I still remember how different it seemed from the United States I knew then. I went to a private school in Wimbledon, several blocks from the famous tennis courts, and gradually became a typical English schoolboy: I wore gray flannel shorts, a gray cotton dress shirt and a solid green tie, a green wool blazer with the circular school emblem on the breast pocket, and a small green cap with the same school emblem sewn on the front. Without even noticing it, I began to speak with an English accent, with far less affectation than people I later met. I learned how to play soccer and cricket, winning an award in the spring for being the "best new cricket player" (meaning, I discovered, the *only* new cricket player).

A decade later, in the late 1960s, after four years of college and a year of graduate school, my fiancée and I were accepted into the fledgling Peace Corps and had to decide where we wanted to go. She had been exposed to Hispanic culture when her family spent several years helping resettle Cuban refugees in New Jersey, and she wanted to experience a different culture. I thought about Asia and talked to my father about his wartime experiences there in the 1940s. He advised against Micronesia: hot, distant, and disease-ridden, at least in his recollections. As we looked at a globe together, he suggested the Philippines instead. It was almost halfway around the world from the East Coast where we lived. Crassly, I figured that if the government was going to pay our way, we might as well go as far away as we could. Africa never crossed my mind.

Two years in the Philippines, along with side trips to Hong Kong, Taiwan, and Japan, sparked an interest in Asian culture. I was lucky to steer clear of Vietnam. The Philippines served well enough to introduce me to this part of the world without having to dodge bullets near the China Sea.

In subsequent years, I had a chance to go back to Europe, this time to lecture and teach on Fulbright grants. I spent a year at the University of Helsinki, followed later by a year at the University of Amsterdam. I enjoyed wandering through the streets of both cities, watching stoic Finns munching sausage rolls in the train station or flower merchants selling tulips along a Dutch canal. I loved listening to the lilt of the Finnish language spoken by shop-keepers at the outdoor market by the Baltic Sea. I even liked hearing the gut-tural Dutch that seemed to come from the deep recesses of the throats of my friends.

My only experience with Africa in all those years came when I was a high-school student, chosen to appear on the *Dorothy Gordon Youth Forum*—a tel-evision show in New York City aimed at letting students meet public officials and talk about the major issues of the day. Our subject, in those preindepen-dence years, was the country called the Belgian Congo, and we spoke about it in stilted and stuffy terms, without any sense of the lasting legacy of colo-nialism or the antagonisms revolving around the question of race. Our dis-cussion was framed by the blinders of the early 1960s and promptly disap-peared from my mind. Years later, I still knew very little about the continent.

Until I met Sara. She was the science librarian at Earlham College, about a half hour away from Miami University in Ohio where I taught. A biologist by training, she sparkled when talking about helping people examine the natural world. Divorced a few years before, she had agreed to take Earlham students on a semester-long study abroad program in Kenya. Since she had once gone to Kenya on a game-park safari, she was presumed to know more than most others about the country. Africa seemed to fill a void in her life, and Kenya provided both a chance to work closely with students struggling to understand a new culture and an opportunity to meet new people—from researchers to expatriates to rural Kenyans living in remote villages far from Nairobi—who became important parts of her life.

In our first encounter, at the home of friends, Sara talked about having drinks on the veranda of the United Kenya Club in Nairobi, the first inte-grated organization in colonial Kenya, and taking students to Lamu, a largely Muslim island on the Indian Ocean near the Somalian border. Her expansive glow made me want to learn more. We traded stories about living and work-ing overseas. I, too, was recently divorced, and we began to see more of each other. Then, barely six weeks after we met, she returned to Kenya for six months, to lead another group of students on a semester abroad.

On her return home, our relationship resumed and, when she announced that she planned to spend the following summer back in Kenya, I decided to go with her for a while. Such a trip was more expensive than I had antici-pated, so I first taught summer school to pay for most of it, borrowed the rest of the money I required, and headed to Africa. Together, we visited Nairobi National Park, visible from the airport as you land, went to Lamu for several days, and climbed Mt. Kenya, the second-tallest mountain in Africa. A fort-night in Kenya was all it took. I managed to avoid malaria but caught a harder-to-shake bug. Africa was in my blood.

More trips followed. In the summer of 1991, Sara and I went back for a month and a half. This time my children, Jenny and David, came for part of the time, and we trekked together up Africa's tallest mountain—Mt. Kilimanjaro in Tanzania—battling altitude sickness, rain, and exhaustion on the way to the top. Sara and I made a trip on our own to Lake Manyara, Tarangire, and the Ngorongoro Crater, all game parks in Tanzania, and then explored the island of Zanzibar, wandering through Stone Town, with its narrow streets and hidden alleys built centuries before, and later hiking the craggy outcroppings along the rocky coast. In 1995, after we were married, we returned to Kenya for a year. Sara had volunteered to lead another college study-abroad program, and I received another Fulbright grant to teach American history for a year at the University of Nairobi. This was a chance to spend an extended time in Africa together, to learn to speak Kiswahili, the national language, and to explore other parts of this seductive land.

What follows is the story of those encounters. As I lived in Kenya and traveled throughout the continent, I learned more about the region—and about myself. Like many Americans, at the outset I regarded Africa in stereotypical terms that, had I thought about it, were straight out of a Tarzan movie or a Joseph Conrad novel: a dark and foreboding place, a damp, dank jungle where my safety was in doubt. I had no sense of its enormous size—four times larger than the United States. Indeed, if you totaled the mass of China, India, Argentina, New Zealand, Europe (minus the former Soviet Union and European Turkey) and the United States, Africa was still larger. Nor was I aware of its tremendous diversity, each of its dozens of countries different from the others, most made up of a variety of ethnic groups as well. Africa is, in historian Basil Davidson's phrase in *The Black Man's Burden: Africa and the Curse of the Nation-State*, "a huge and hugely complex continent."

As a white American making my first visit to Africa in 1990, I was vaguely intimidated by the idea of entering an all-black world. I had lived with black roommates in college, taught with black colleagues throughout my teaching career, and enjoyed a number of close black friends. At the same time, when I had volunteered in some of Boston's black communities during my undergraduate years, I had always felt like an outsider. Now I was dealing with an even greater sense of what it is like to be in the minority.

My arrival in Nairobi on my very first trip only reinforced my initial anxiety. In the Jomo Kenyatta Airport, all the officials were black—airline agents, custodians, customs clerks. Passing through the immigration bureaucracy seemed like a slow motion dream. More than in other countries I had visited, I wanted to be sure that I did everything right. I hoped I would not have to explain away any inadvertent problems, out of a naive fear that my white skin would cause me trouble by making me stand out.

As I finally stumbled into the large waiting area at about 5 A.M., I was relieved that Sara, who had arrived several weeks earlier, was waiting with a jeep. She steered clear of the crowd, counseled me to trust British Airways, and promised I would get my suitcase back. Putting my one remaining bag into the jeep, we set off down the highway back to town. The night was clear, and savannah-like fields bordering Nairobi National Park unfolded as we left the airport. In years past, animals roamed this terrain, sometimes even wandering across the road. Now civilization made it less likely that we would see lions or giraffes as we drove along, although some of these animals are frequently visible from the air.

About twenty minutes later, we reached Nairobi with its population of a million people, a big city by East African standards. It looked like other cities I have known. Neon lights glittered like welcoming lanterns, creating a reddish glow. Small skyscrapers soared over what I later learned was Uhuru Park, a green belt cutting the city in two. Vehicles sped by us, even in the hours before dawn. It was comforting to feel that Kenya might not be as strange as I had first thought and that I might be on relatively familiar turf after all.

Like so much that unfolded in the next weeks and months and years, my reaction was a serious misperception. Parts of Kenya—and Africa—*appear* deceptively familiar, but are rarely what they seem. Look further, and you realize how different ordinary things really are. And even when you know they are different, you are still surprised by what you find.

Africa was an adventure. Not like the escapades of Theodore Roosevelt and other big game hunters who shot the wildlife and then left with the bounty of their grisly craft. Not like the explorations of Isak Dinesen and other European settlers who sailed halfway around the world, started large farms that Africans tended, and came to call Kenya their home. For me, the adventure was an interior journey in an ever-changing land, as I began to wonder about the patterns of African life and to question how they differed from my own.

Over time, as I began to feel more comfortable in my surroundings, I began to ask people about issues that puzzled me. I talked to taxi drivers, colleagues at the university, embassy officials, neighbors, and friends. Some spoke to me in formal interviews and answered questions I asked; others simply chatted with me, either in the Kiswahili language I was struggling to learn or in English that all Kenyans study in school. Slowly, over the course of our stay, I became more familiar with the contours of the country, and, as we traveled elsewhere, with patterns that were visible, even if in somewhat different form, in other African countries as well.

The more I listened and learned, the more I came to understand that, although most Americans know very little about the continent, Africa is unavoidable today. And that our ignorance bears a huge price. Rwanda burst upon the world scene in 1994 as a brutal civil war resulted in the gory deaths of more than

500,000 innocent people, a genocide that the United States and its allies wouldn't confront. Burundi remains in the news as it faces the same bloody fate. Somalia became better known as American soldiers participated in a futile and ill-informed effort to aid the victims of a terrible famine and to pacify local warlords rampaging out of control. South Africa, one of the great success stories of recent years that we like to point to, has freed itself of almost half a century of apartheid, but is still in the midst of the stupefyingly difficult task of making the transition to a multiracial democracy. And, as the world community has begun to realize, while AIDS is a worldwide disease, it has hit sub-Saharan Africa worst of all. Kenya, traditionally more stable than many other African nations, faces many of the same problems as its own stability erodes.

My own safari—the Kiswahili word for any journey—unfolded as I struggled to understand my surroundings. Sometimes the route was uncertain, as I made innocent cross-cultural mistakes that are part of learning to live in any land. I'm sure I offended some of my hosts by not taking a second helping of food or by not drinking enough beer or tea. But those occasionally awkward interactions paled against the larger uncertainty I perceived in the Kenya I came to appreciate. Kenya's government, both under first President Jomo Kenyatta and then under strong-armed Daniel arap Moi, who has only just relinquished power, has long been mired in corruption, the magnitude of which is only beginning to be realized today. The roads are among the worst I've seen in Africa, and the infrastructure—viewed with pride in colonial days—is crumbling. Nearly one in ten Kenyans is infected with the HIV virus, and the full-blown AIDS disease is devastating schools, colleges, and other public and private institutions, with more than 500 deaths a day. Kenya had tremendous promise when it attained independence in 1963, but, in the decades that followed, it has suffered one setback after another and, despite its beauty and boundless sense of possibility, its stability remains fragile. Kenya today, with a new government, is embarking on its own uncertain safari in its struggle to survive.

The longer I lived in Kenya, the more I wanted the country to succeed, and I usually tried to avoid dwelling on what sometimes seemed insoluble issues, to understand but not to obsess. In any event, much of my time was spent transacting the details of daily life. I had classes to teach, essays to write, Kiswahili words to learn. For all the occasional frustrations, unavoidable in any developing land, and my larger fears about the fate of the nation, the experience was a rich and rewarding one. I came to feel the passion for Africa that Sara had conveyed when we first met, and I came to love Kenya as much as she did. I have tried to capture some of that feeling in what is meant as an affectionate portrait of people, places, and problems, filled with small particulars and personal stories that will, I hope, illuminate larger issues in Kenya—and Africa—today.

The Necessities of Life

I started my extended stay in Africa searching for a place to live. Sara and I arrived in Kenya in mid-July 1995, with a few weeks of free time before her students appeared and she had to go to work. My own teaching assignment at the University of Nairobi was not scheduled to begin for two months, but I felt a need to settle down immediately, to find a place I could call home, and, in the process, to make the adjustment to living in Africa and not just passing through a foreign land. Sara was less impatient, for she was going to be spending the first part of her year with her students in various locations around the country. She would be coming in and out of Nairobi, but was not staying for good until the end of the semester.

According to the terms of my Fulbright grant, the university was supposed to provide me with an apartment. But, I soon learned, expectation and reality do not always correspond. There *was* a flat available in a housing complex for faculty and staff members, located about a ten minute walk from the university — and the center of Nairobi. This apartment, I found, was often occupied by visitors from abroad. An American Fulbright professor had lived there for a year in the past. Right now, an academic from Zambia, who had been there for a couple of months, was about to return home.

To me, it seemed as though the issue was settled. I could move in as soon as my predecessor moved out. Immediately, I felt a vast sense of relief.

It quickly became clear, however, that the whole situation was more complicated than I first realized. While my Fulbright award had been approved by a dozen committees in Kenya and the United States, the University of Nairobi had not given the final approval for my appointment. It did not seem to matter that the university had *requested* the appointment in the first place. Or that both the history department and the university administration had signed off when the Fulbright Commission shared my application with authorities in Nairobi prior to notifying me of my award. Formal approval from the University Council was necessary before I became an official member of the academic community. And that might take weeks — or months. As I began to wonder whether the problem might ever get resolved, I got a sinking feeling in my stomach.

I didn't know what to do. I tried to rely on the director of housing, who told me to be patient. But patience is harder for me in a foreign country, where differences loom large and I long for a few familiar signposts to reassure myself that everything is going to be all right.

Like many Americans, I was always itching to get on with presumably important tasks. I wanted to move smoothly from one assignment to the next, to accomplish my objectives, to get things done. I prided myself on my ability to function, and, until now, my environment had rewarded me for my performance, even if the pressure to perform sometimes made me feel like an inflated balloon ready to pop. My first job was to resolve the issue of housing. After that, I could move on to the next item on the checklist in my mind.

I tried to relax by telling myself that Sara and I were not really hurting yet. We were staying at the United Kenya Club, which serves as both a hotel for academic visitors and a social club for a cross-section of intellectual, business, and political leaders in Kenya. We found it comfortable and exciting, sitting on the veranda, chatting with other guests, sipping "gin tonics" or bottles of Tusker beer. I liked the United Kenya Club, which, like everyone else, I called the UKC. But even my most earnest efforts to accept eagerly all that Kenya offered could not disguise the fact that the drapes were ripped, the rugs frayed, the floor worn. Most of the lampshades were broken and many of the lights didn't work. I had found the rooms charming in the past, when I returned for a day or two after a safari. Now the prospect of a year in a shabby hotel room seemed discouraging.

My fears of being forgotten by the university, as I waited for the bureaucracy to decide I belonged, were not entirely ungrounded. Another Fulbright professor and her family, who arrived a few months after we did, ended up in just that situation. They lived in a different hotel for weeks on end, until they asked for an assignment in another country and, thereby, pushed the bureaucrats to find them an adequate place to live.

Almost immediately after arriving in Africa, I had met Macharia, a faculty member in the history department at the University of Nairobi. He had been educated in the United States, receiving his Ph.D. at Ohio University, close to my own institution. As we talked about our respective experiences in Africa and America, he seemed to straddle both cultures. He was sensitive to my plight and evidently knew how to proceed.

Most Kenyans, when faced with such a problem, seem inclined to wait for something to happen, rather than take matters into their own hands. The bureaucracy may move slowly, but they let it run its course. When clerks hesitate to take any action, usually out of fear that they will be called to account for their deeds, most people simply wait quietly for something to happen, however long that takes.

Impatient, I thought: When in doubt, go to the top. And so I asked Macharia to take me to see the vice chancellor. He blanched. I repeated my request. How else would I be able to get the necessary permission to move into an apartment that was available now but might be given to someone else in the future? Didn't I stand to lose the apartment if I waited for the University Council to meet, with no meeting scheduled in the foreseeable future?

Macharia's reluctance stemmed from his awareness of the power structure at the university. The president of Kenya at that time, Daniel arap Moi, was chancellor of the University of Nairobi and every other national university in Kenya. The vice chancellor owed his appointment to the president and worked closely with him, sometimes on a daily basis. He—and the president —could fire faculty members at will, and indeed had done so several years ago when a strike for higher wages closed the entire university system down. The vice chancellor was a man of means, to be treated with courtesy and respect. I was naively asking Macharia to do something that could have hidden costs.

Still, Macharia recognized my problem and proved willing to help—or at least to humor me. Perhaps it was an innate Kenyan courtesy that made him willing to take a risk, the magnitude of which I only later understood. Together, Sara, Macharia, and I went to the vice chancellor's office. Fortunately for us, he was in and was willing to see us. We waited for a time in an outer office, watching secretaries work on old Macintosh computers, an uncomfortable silence filling the room. At last we were ushered in. Macharia, whom we had seen earlier as outgoing and expansive, was much more subdued as we entered the paneled office. The vice chancellor put us at our ease. He, too, had studied in the United States, and we chatted amiably about different programs. Finally, he asked us how he could help. I wondered if he might be able to notify the housing department that I was a legitimate university employee and authorize the release of the one available apartment to us before it was given away to someone else. The vice chancellor nodded. That was no problem, he said. He would speak to one of his assistants, and I could get the necessary authorization later in the day.

It was not that simple. After a number of attempts, I managed to locate the vice chancellor's assistant. It took time for the necessary letter to be prepared. When I eventually got it, the housing director seemed reluctant to accept it because this was a breach of protocol. Finally, she agreed that we could have the flat, largely, I suppose, to keep me from coming back to bother her again.

My persistence proved more important than I had imagined. About a month later, before the University Council met, the chairman of that board was killed in a car crash. During an extended period of mourning, little business was transacted. I never did get the official notification of my appointment in the entire time I was in Kenya. Had I not insisted on something happening when I did, we might have stayed at the UKC.

My difficulties in finding a flat should have warned me of other pitfalls that lay ahead. But I learned the wrong lesson from this episode and remained naively optimistic that I could handle anything. After all, I had found us a place to live. On to the next task.

The apartment itself looked inviting when we moved in. It was light and airy, with a large window offering a view of the Nairobi skyline and Uhuru Park. It had a living room, a dining room I used as a study, two bedrooms, and a kitchen. Much to my delight, it had a shower with hot and cold running water and electricity providing light in all the rooms. Best of all, the flat had a phone. And there were other amenities as well. One balcony off the kitchen had a large sink and room for laundry, if we wanted to wash our clothes by hand. Another balcony off the living room afforded an open-air city view. We began to dream of sitting there, drinks in hand, watching the sun go down. Not all views, however, were quite as enticing. From each corner of the flat, we could look down at a different garbage dump. One large bin was burning at the time. I later learned that was the way most garbage was disposed of. Each bin would get increasingly full before being burned, attracting hungry crows and stray cats that rummaged through the debris.

Our neighbor Charles spoke knowingly about rainwater leaks as we settled in. He had come as a Fulbright fellow and stayed on for the past three years, living in the apartment immediately below. The apartments were not well built, he told me. Poor planning had been compounded by poor construction. The university ran out of money before it finished the complex. The most serious problems faced those of us living on the top floor.

As I looked around, I noticed what Charles was talking about. Several walls had pockmarks on them, with splotches that looked like they had been made from the residue of a gunpowder shell. In the bedroom, the light-colored paint had begun to peel and crumble, leaving a pasty powder where there had once been smooth stretches of white. The basic problem was the leaky roof, but another problem was the walls, which proved as porous as a sponge if the rain came from the north.

I had already learned enough to know that trying to get the university to paint the apartment was not a possibility. It might get done, though even that was doubtful, but long after I was gone. I had also quickly learned that there were far greater priorities at the university, which would also never get met, than painting an apartment. With a growing sense of how fortunate we were, Sara and I decided to have the apartment painted ourselves at our own expense. We quickly got an estimate of about $300, a small fortune in Kenya, but reasonable for us. And the painters, elated at having work, were willing to come the next day.

A few weeks later, our flat looked brand new. After we hung curtains on the windows and put a colorful carpet on the floor, the apartment seemed cozy and warm. With a silkscreen picture of a roadside scene by Robin Anderson, a prominent Kenyan artist, on one wall, and other treasures from the market scattered in odd corners and on shelves, it felt like home—a home that we would never again take for granted as our due.

As the year wore on, there were occasional water leaks, and slowly the bedroom wall began to deteriorate again. But the ominous warning Charles had given about a flood on the floor receded in my mind. I laughed it off, especially as my stay in Kenya was drawing to an end. Then one July evening, when the rainy season was supposed to be over, Nairobi was caught in a terrible storm. The streets filled with huge pools of water, stopping cars like spiders stuck in a sodden web, as drivers splashing through large puddles flooded their distributors and slowed to a halt. Sara and I headed off to the airport to pick up some friends, feeling lucky that our car continued to run. The plane was several hours late, and so we returned home to take a nap before checking at the airport again. As we entered the apartment, we found three inches of water on the floor. And, until the rain stopped, it kept pouring in through a small hole in the bathroom wall that must have been connected to a channel behind the plaster, which was in turn connected to a leak in the roof. Without even looking at one another, Sara and I grabbed towels and buckets, and dropped to our knees on the floor. Three hours and dozens of gallons of water later, we had the apartment relatively dry, just in time to head back to the airport.

Water became a motif in my life, as it was in the lives of all Kenyans. Water was the lifeblood of the country. But, unlike in the United States, where we take for granted turning on the hot-water spigot in the shower or doing the wash in a machine, water was not always easy to obtain. That was true upcountry, miles from Nairobi. It turned out to be true in the city as well.

Early in our stay, Sara's students spent several days living with the Maasai, a pastoral people whose lives revolve around herding cattle and goats, and I joined them for the better part of that stay. Sara and some of her students went off with the women one morning to get water. It involved a healthy trek down to the river, then an even harder walk back uphill, each with a large plastic can on her back, hung from a strap on her head. The pattern proved to be countrywide.

When I visited Sara and her students in Kaimosi, another rural area near Lake Victoria, about six hours from Nairobi, the students were living with families that did not always have running water inside. Sara and I were staying in a Quaker guest house, with water faucets in several rooms promising a constant supply. I had been told about the impressive water system built by Quaker missionaries early in this century and could see ceramic pipes near the surface of the soil as we walked down the main dirt road. But each day, at indeterminate times, the water went off. Maybe there was a shortage. Maybe the water was being parceled out to other areas as part of a rationing scheme. Maybe the system had finally fallen apart. I never knew.

The only way to cook or bathe or flush the toilet was to fill twenty-gallon cans when the water was on. I went out to a hardware store fifteen miles away to buy the necessary containers. I became adept at rushing to a spigot as soon as the water supply returned, to keep the cans full. After a while, I began to feel proud of myself for learning to handle the water problems in the village.

Then I returned to Nairobi. For the first few months, the water had run regularly. Showers were pleasant and hot. The pressure was good. It was just like home. But now, everything changed. Sometime in November, the water company began to cut the water off, at odd hours, often for half a day at a time. At first it was nothing to worry about. There were tanks up on the roof—above our fourth-floor apartment—and as long as we had pressure for a while, the tanks filled up and we had water to use for the rest of the day.

Then the water pressure started to disappear for two days at a time. And then for three.

By December, the situation had become desperate, and I had begun to rely on a bucket brigade. Every couple of days, I descended four flights of stairs, walked over to an open spigot several hundred meters away, and filled a large plastic container with water. Then I passed it on to a friend or neighbor or hauled it back up the stairs myself, wondering why those Maasai women never complained.

To wash myself, I learned to squat in the shower, take a sponge bath in a tiny pail of water, wondering if or when the pressure would return. It was fun the first time, a burden the next. After several weeks, I was ready to move somewhere else, but there was nowhere to go.

Water, I came to realize, is a serious problem confronting all Kenyans. Some areas in Eastern Province, or in the Turkana District in the north, get virtually no rain. Pastoralists wander from place to place in search of food and what little water they can find for their cattle. But when periodic drought strikes, they have a hard time even scraping out that meager existence. Other

Kenyans suffer from the huge population explosion that has sorely tested the infrastructure of the country. Water supplies that were sufficient in the past are no longer adequate in a nation with one of the highest rates of population growth in the world. And efforts to build dams to increase the water supply become mired in the corruption that compromises all efforts to get ahead.

It's not just water. We began to encounter trouble with the power as well. The electricity was pretty reliable for most of our stay. With transformers for a couple of special appliances we had brought from home, we were able to use the Kenyan 220-volt current without much trouble. The power would flicker off frequently for a few moments at a time, several times a day. Still, I could work around any problems. I kept a supply of candles on hand to provide light when the electricity failed and came to enjoy gazing at the flickering flame.

Indeed, I felt fortunate when I spoke to Harvey, an American professor of architecture who had been living in Kenya for the past ten years. He had moved into our complex sometime before we had arrived, and told me about his problem with the current. Every evening, at around 6:00 P.M., his power went out. Perhaps there was a shortage. Maybe his flat served as a kind of safety valve, allowing all of the rest of us in the building to enjoy the light. Whatever the reason, Harvey found himself regularly in the dark. And so he took to calling the Kenya Power and Light Company, which, like all our neighbors and friends, we came to call the Kenya Power and Darkness Company, complaining until the electricity came back on.

Eventually, the authorities became tired of Harvey's calls. And so, toward the end of our stay, as his power remained on, *our* power began to go off every evening, just around dinner time. Like Harvey earlier, we had to cook in the late afternoon, if we wanted to use our electric oven and stove. And, like Harvey, I learned how to call the power company hot line, get transferred from one person to another until I could state my case, accept assurances that the power would return shortly, and then sit by candlelight, hoping that things might return to normal before we went to bed.

Power, like water, is in short supply all over Kenya. Rural Kenyans, living in small huts, do not have electricity. But others, residing in more developed villages and towns, may enjoy only an intermittent supply. The huge Turkwel Gorge dam project north of Kitale in the west was supposed to provide a large percentage of the power in a nationwide grid. But the dam never filled up as expected. When I visited the project in 1996, one of the two generators was disassembled, as engineers waited for months for replacement parts, and the other was off-line. Upon asking when it might be working again, I received the generic answer I came to expect to any such question: Soon.

The problems with electricity were nothing compared to difficulties with the phone. I knew from past trips to Africa that it was often hard to make a call. Trying to make phone contact with outlying areas was like yelling into a canyon and taking a chance that someone at the bottom might hear you and respond. Reaching another person in Nairobi was sometimes just as difficult. The phone might give you a busy signal, even though it was not in use. Or it might play a recording, in both Kiswahili and English, telling you the number you wanted was out of service, even though you had spoken on the same line just moments ago. Or you might get cut off in the middle of a conversation, and then find it impossible to reconnect to continue the call.

My pleasure at finding an apartment with a telephone had been quickly punctured when I realized the phone did not work. During a trip to the Post Office, which ran all telecommunications in the country, I learned that I had to deal directly with a university office since we lived in a university flat. I groaned at the thought of facing the institutional bureaucracy again. Fortunately, I was able to avoid going back to the housing office. But now I had to find out where to go instead. It took a day to locate the university's telecommunications center. Its phone was working, but a secretary told me that it was better for me to show up in person if I wanted to get anything done. And so, the next day, I went to the university's telecom center promptly at 8:00 A.M. to wait for a man named Rick.

Rick showed up about twenty minutes later, and promised to help. He checked with the Post Office, arranged to have service resumed, and promised to send a couple of his assistants to the flat to make sure everything worked. All I needed to do was return to the apartment and wait. Was someone going to come right away? He reassured me that he would send help as quickly as he could.

Reluctantly, I went back home, wondering if this was going to entail another series of interminable delays. Soon, however, the doorbell rang, and two workmen came to look at the phone. They checked to see that the line had indeed been turned back on, but then reported the bad news that the telephone itself needed repair. Fortunately, I had brought a fax machine with me to Kenya, in the naive expectation that it could keep me in touch with people back home. The workmen quickly wired the fax machine into the phone line and, much to my relief, we got a dial tone. I breathed a sigh of relief.

They told me to take the telephone itself back to Rick and ask for a replacement. When I did, Rick responded that there were no replacements; equipment at the University of Nairobi was in short supply. But he pulled out a screwdriver, put the phone on his desk and pulled it apart, and an hour later was able to make it work. Then he told me I needed to get the workmen back to wire *this* phone into our line, so that we could use it as well as the fax machine. There were, apparently, no jacks or plugs that could run two lines into one box. All the wiring had to be done by hand.

Half a day later, the job was complete. My phone and fax machine both worked. Now I could make and receive calls, as long as the connections with the rest of the country—and the world—remained intact. I learned later that there was a new line called AT&T Direct, which established almost instant contact with the United States. For a small price, at least by American standards, I could simply dial a number and reach the AT&T operator at home. Much to my surprise, it was easier to call my daughter in Seattle or my son in Los Angeles than to reach a neighbor in Nairobi only two blocks away.

Over the course of the year, I often wondered about the importance I attached to the phone. Back home, I relied on the telephone to stay in touch with colleagues and friends. Instead of writing a letter, I often called. I had voice mail to take messages in my office and an answering machine at home. The phone served me—and so many other Americans—as a kind of crutch. In my life in the United States, the telephone helped bring people closer, and served as a substitute for extended family ties.

Such connections were impossible in Kenya. Internal phone systems worked in the large multinational corporations and banks. But ordinary businesses faced the same obstacles I encountered. Like virtually all Kenyans, I had to scale down my expectations.

Just as I was getting confident I had everything I needed to function in Kenya, the phone went dead. Entirely dead. I realized that my adjustment was not as deep-rooted as I had thought. For as soon as the dial tone disappeared, I felt the recurrence of all of the anxieties I had been trying to suppress. Had I done something wrong? Had I failed to make a deposit? Was there a larger problem I knew nothing about? Was this was part of a persistent pattern that would plague me for the remainder of my stay?

My fears proved well-founded. When I went back to Rick, I discovered that the Zambian tenant who had preceded us had not paid his telephone bill. There was a forwarding address, to be sure, but no telephone number. And, Rick told me, there was little chance of being able to track him down and make him pay. Africa simply didn't work that way. Rick gave me a glance that said, "I know you can handle this," as he told me that if I wanted to get the phone service to resume, *I* was going to have to pay the bill. I thought about it for a moment, and then I took out my wallet and gave Rick the money. I needed to feel connected to the rest of the world. The telephone was my lifeline to all the people I knew, even if it didn't always work. Rick authorized one of his assistants to carry the cash across town to the Post Office, with an urgent request to a friend of his there to turn the phone back on. Otherwise it might take days or weeks for service to resume.

The same thing happened the next month. Now I learned that there was a long time lag between service and bills. Earlier, I had paid for our Zambian friend's *June* calls. To get the phone service restored again, I would also have to pay for *July*. Once again, I forked over the money, and the magical dial tone returned.

A few months later, Sara and I lost our phone service once more. This time the problem was that the university bureaucracy had not distributed bills until *after* the date the payment was due. All university phone service was cut off and took days to resume.

Things changed dramatically in subsequent years. With the advent of mobile phones, Kenya, like countries around the world, moved quickly into the digital age. Today, you can't walk down a street in Nairobi, or sit in a restaurant or a shop, without watching someone make a call. Middle- and upper-class Kenyans are the ones with the phones, to be sure. But even people living in humble surroundings without permanent jobs sometimes have cell phones, activated with cards they can purchase when they have the necessary funds. They recognize that a phone can be essential if they ever hope to move ahead.

Even before the cell-phone explosion, there *were* other ways to communicate with the world outside. As I headed overseas, I had thought I might be able to use the Internet to stay in touch. Sara and I had both become addicted to e-mail at home, and relied on it to contact colleagues and friends. Computers were coming to Africa, I knew, and at a Fulbright orientation conference, I learned that some countries were already providing on-line service for a price.

In the past, the Kenyan government had made it difficult, even impossible, to carry computers into the country. Political power depended on keeping tight control over the means of communication. Some machines, according to possibly apocryphal stories, were confiscated at the Jomo Kenyatta Airport or inexplicably lost at the Mombasa port. Others were assessed a 100 percent import duty that had to be paid on the spot. But by 1995, apparently, restrictions had eased. With proper documentation that my computer belonged to me and would accompany me on my return home, I would be able to bring it in.

As we collected our eleven bags and boxes at the airport in Nairobi and trudged toward the customs line, I did my best to appear casual. Be honest, I told myself, but be firm. When the official asked me if I was carrying any electronic equipment, I nodded, told him I had a fax machine and computer for personal use, and looked him squarely in the eye. Much to my relief, he waved me on.

Getting the computer into the country was easy; getting it connected to the outside world was a nightmare. With the aid of a transformer, I got plugged in to the power supply—when it worked—but I wanted Internet access as well. Our neighbor Charles told us there was a company downtown called Omega that could hook us up to an e-mail outfit known as Thorn Tree and, as soon as we were settled into our apartment, I went to see what could be done.

I had problems from the start. Kenya, I learned, was most comfortable with IBMs or comparable machines. I had used an IBM for the past ten years, but had just splurged and bought a new Macintosh PowerBook before coming to Africa, admiring its versatility and thinking it might be easier to service abroad. Now I learned that Macs were scarce and it was going to take some effort to make the new machine work.

My first encounters at Omega produced few positive results. I walked up a narrow staircase, down a cluttered corridor, and finally found the appropriate door. An expatriate American named Ron quickly signed me up and took my money. But when African technicians tried to install the necessary communications software in my machine, it quickly became clear they did not know how the Mac worked. I watched them struggle most of one afternoon, then another. Finally, in frustration, they referred me to a new Apple dealer several blocks away.

The Apple dealership was a real contrast to Omega. It boasted a well-supplied storefront overlooking Uhuru Park. It was stocked with piles of new machines. An Indian family ran the establishment, and I was quickly referred to Riaz, one of the owners, who apparently knew just what to do. He logged off his own machine, which looked just like mine, installed the appropriate software, and showed me how to connect to a new account. Everything worked, at least until I got home.

For the next four weeks, I labored in vain to get on-line. Sometimes I could connect, but then the software package seemed to self-destruct. One or two messages arrived from home, but they only told me that most of what I sent never got through. I went back to Riaz time and again, endlessly bolstered by his cheery optimism, increasingly disturbed by my inability to make things work.

Meanwhile, my quest to get on-line had become like a search for the Holy Grail. I *knew* it had to work somehow. I simply didn't know where to look or whom to ask for help. Rather than get impatient, Sara humored me. She had her students' problems on her mind, and my effort at high-tech communication seemed fanciful at best, given her own experience with how the country worked. In my more lucid moments, I had to acknowledge that I did not really *need* this Internet connection at all. I had done all right without it in the past. I was now in Africa, where no one at home expected me to remain in close touch. It was more a reflection of my own insecurity at being away for an extended period of time that drove me on, even when Sara quietly assured me that we could manage just fine even if e-mail never got through.

Reluctantly, I gave up the quest. I would manage as most other visitors had for the past hundred years. I began to write real letters, faxing some, sending others with stamps. Then, a month or so later, I drove a couple of friends and their son out to the International School of Kenya for a parent-teacher conference. While they spoke to the teachers, I wandered over to the library, to see what kind of computer equipment the institution used. I saw Mac after Mac in what looked just like an American computer lab. When I asked about e-mail access, I was referred to an American teacher named Leon, who ran the computer center. He was conversant with the latest software packages and proudly showed me the system he ran. When I gingerly broached the question of whether I could join for a fee, he said why not. By the next day, I was on-line and ready to go.

It was worth the wait. Messages came through regularly, as long as I could dial in. Of course, dialing in sometimes posed problems, since there was only one phone line to the server, and it was often in use. Finally, I found that if I got up at 5:00 A.M., well before most students awoke, I could usually manage to get through.

Computer access did improve in the next few years. When I returned to Kenya the following summer, I found it possible, even easy, to hook up to the World Wide Web, through a company called Africa Online. By the time Sara and I returned in 2003 with another group of students to lead on a semester abroad, we were able to connect our laptop to a mobile phone and dial in that way.

But in 1995, though affluent Kenyans could afford computers, most people communicated by ordinary post. And so did I. Although I preferred to avoid it, I had to venture frequently to the main Post Office, off by the railroad station. It looked like a huge cavern with most of the residents of Nairobi huddled inside. More conveniently located, but no less crowded, were several branch offices scattered around the city. As with everything else I did in Kenya, going to the Post Office took a lot of time.

Mailing a letter was the easy part. The first time I tried to buy stamps, there were only a dozen people in line ahead of me. Patiently, I inched my way toward the clerk, politely but firmly resisting interlopers—even clergy in religious dress—who tried to push ahead of me. Just as I reached the window, the person ahead of me pulled out a pile of fifty letters, all of which needed to be individually weighed.

Mailing a package was even harder. After waiting in line for half an hour one day at the substation near the university, I discovered, to my dismay, that I could only mail overseas packages from the main Post Office. Since I needed to dispatch a small packet containing one of my American doctoral student's dissertation chapters, I had no choice but to head over there.

I hoped the process would be as easy as mailing a letter. I had wrapped the package nicely, with staples and tape, and was ready to send it on its way. But now I found other obstacles stood in the way. First I had to take the packet to a customs window. The clerk told me—in Kiswahili—to open it so she could see it. I did. The chapter—undoubtedly worth thousands of dollars to my student—had no commercial value at all. Yet I still had to fill out a customs waiver, to paste on the package itself.

But now the package was no longer sealed. And I had left the staples and tape back home. So I had to leave the Post Office, buy supplies elsewhere, and return to try again. After waiting in another long line, I found that it would cost $25 to mail a package that would cost about $5 in the United States. But what could I do?

This effort paled beside the effort it took to *pick up* a package. The first time I tried, it took three-quarters of an hour, and I had to go to eight different windows before I was able to leave.

First, I had to go upstairs at the main Post Office to another large room, showing guards along the way the little yellow slip telling me that a package had arrived. I waited at one window while a clerk looked in a holding area for my parcel. Finally, he returned with a box, but that was only the start. Then I had to take it to another window, open it in front of another clerk, and have him decide if I had to pay duty. Then on to still another clerk to fill out a duty form, and to another to make sure the first clerk had filled out the form correctly, and then to the cashier to pay the money, and then to a supervisor to review all the preceding paperwork. And each window required a wait in line until it was my turn.

Done, I said to myself as I moved away from the last window. I was wrong. I came to still one more clerk, and now I had to surrender the original little yellow slip that told me I had a package to pick up. But I had lost the slip en route. And so I had to retrace my steps to all the other windows, dutifully waiting in line, until I located the elusive paper and could return it at last.

I managed to communicate with the outside world with patience and persistence, and a little bit of luck. I came to rely on the electronic connections, when they worked, for they made it easier to remain in touch with colleagues and friends back home, and to meet deadlines that were still part of my life. But I also came to accept more traditional means when I had no other choice.

In the process, I came to appreciate the importance of quick and reliable communication if economic development is ever going to occur. Kenya, though it now has skyscrapers and too many cars, looks much like it did decades ago. You can buy flowers—and snacks and souvenirs—from hawkers on the streets. Merchants talk pleasantly with you when you venture into a store. People move at a slower pace and savor their relationships with family members and friends in the course of their daily lives. There are no cow-herding nomads in Nairobi, to be sure, but country customs still govern at least some of the patterns of city life. At the same time, Kenya wants to develop economically, to avoid being left behind as more prosperous Western nations zoom ahead. With CNN available virtually everywhere, Kenyans— and other Africans—have a much better sense than ever before of what the world is like outside. Yet problems with infrastructure undermine the stability that is necessary for real development to take place.

We can joke about inadequate sources of water or problems with the power supply. These stories circulate around the country, told by residents and visitors both. Kenyans—and their friends—learn to cope, for they have no other choice. But tourism, which is now Kenya's largest source of income, suffers as a result. Investors, both from within Kenya and from abroad, need to be able to communicate quickly with others in the same way they can in other parts of the world, or they take their money elsewhere.

Midway through my stay in Kenya, I attended a meeting at the University of Nairobi with former Secretary of Commerce Ron Brown. He was in Africa with a group of American businessmen, trying to interest them in the possibility of large-scale investment in a number of sub-Saharan countries. Many of the members of the entourage were African Americans, who wanted to connect with African nations out of a sense of solidarity with a continent that was once their forebears' home. But they recognized the sometimes insurmountable problems of doing business in a part of the world where the infrastructure was falling apart, and it was not at all clear they were going to make the large commitments the Secretary of Commerce sought. Brown may have made modest inroads before his untimely death in a plane crash in the Balkans, but he still had a long way to go.

As I learned to cope with the problems of water, power, and communication, I realized that other tasks also took time. Most important was the mundane process of buying food. Some things were easy to get. I could leave our flat and wander over to a line of small *dukas*—open-air booths—just a few feet away. They were ramshackle structures, some as simple as a number of random boards hammered together over a pile of stones. Several sold rich green avocados, ripe pineapples, fresh bananas, and other items we could eat on the spot. Another *duka* that looked like a small box, large enough to hold only one or two clerks at a time, sold margarine, eggs, and what we called "nuked milk." It came in small cardboard containers and had been zapped with some kind of radiation so it wouldn't spoil on the shelf. Still another stand sold french fries, so greasy the oil seeped through the thin paper bag they came in and stained my hands and clothes as I wolfed them down, telling myself that cholesterol only counted if consumed in the United States.

For more substantial fare, I had a number of choices. The Uchumi chain of supermarkets (named after the Kiswahili word for economy) had stores throughout the city and in the suburbs. Sara and I relied on these for staples, but preferred to go elsewhere for fruits, vegetables, meats, and breads. In suburban shopping centers that were like small malls, I could find all of these things. And, for the best prices of all, I could go to the city market downtown. There I could bargain with the attendants for fresh produce, hunks of beef, and chickens dead or alive. There was another huge wholesale market just beyond the railroad station that we visited once with a friend. But it was an overwhelming place, with people moving large bags of produce through narrow pathways so quickly that I was afraid of getting knocked down.

Shopping was the easy part. Cooking proved more difficult, especially because Sara and I wanted to learn to prepare Kenyan foods. Fortunately, we lived just across the hall from a colleague in the history department, and Mary soon took pity on the feeble efforts she watched us make.

Mary was a forty-year-old graduate student and lecturer who lived with her two daughters, son, estranged husband, and assorted relatives from her rural up-country home. Her apartment was the same size as ours, and I was embarrassed when I realized that I had worried about having enough room for just Sara and me. Mary had a friendly word for everyone. With a wide smile and a hearty laugh, she quickly became one of our best friends. She worked long hours at the university, teaching courses, grading papers, and trying occasionally to do her own research. Then, at the end of the day, she headed over to United States International University, an American-based institution with a branch in Kenya, to teach still other courses for an additional stipend, for she did not earn enough at the University of Nairobi to survive.

Early in our stay in Kenya, I was alone for a time. While Sara took her students to a number of sites outside Nairobi, I stayed back in the city to do my own work, visiting every week or so whenever I could get away. Though I was used to cooking regularly back home, now I found the whole operation overwhelming, especially since everything had to be done from scratch, and I began to rely on fresh fruit and scrambled eggs most evenings I was alone. Mary stopped by the flat occasionally to make sure I was all right and was horrified by what she saw. Before long, she began to send over *chapatis* (flat, tortilla-like pancakes), *irio* (a mixture of potatoes, cabbage, and beans), *sukuma wiki* (a spinach-like mixture of greens) and a host of other Kenyan foods. Having established a pattern, she never deviated from it, even when Sara returned home. We often opened the door to the flat and found plates of steaming food on the kitchen counter, just waiting to be consumed.

Cooking became easier in time. Once Sara's students went back to the United States, she returned to Nairobi for good. Unlike me, she is adventurous and creative in the kitchen, and quickly became comfortable cooking Kenyan food, as long as the power supply let us use the electric stove.

One of my proudest accomplishments came when we were up-country, and Sara offered to cook a chicken dinner the next day for some friends who were *askaris*, or guards, at the guest house where we were staying. David, one of the *askaris*, offered to provide the meat. That first evening, we heard a clucking at the door. I looked out. There was nothing to be seen. Later, as we sat down to dinner with David and his colleague Elijah, David said in Kiswahili, "We'd better bring the chicken inside." And he walked out the back door, picked up a handsome brown and red hen tied to a post on the porch, brought it into the kitchen, and deposited it on the floor of the kitchen pantry for the night. This, I learned later, was so that local dogs on the prowl would not get our dinner after we had gone to bed.

The next morning, David was at the doorstep at dawn. We were going to kill the chicken, he said. I had heard stories about chickens running around aimlessly after their heads had been cut off, and I wasn't quite sure what to expect.

Deftly, David placed one foot on our hen's feet, and the other on one wing. I helped hold the chicken as he stretched the neck out along the ground, and with one quick stroke of our knife, he slit the neck. Within seconds, the bird was dead. It quivered a bit, but then, mercifully, expired in my hands. Quickly we dipped the chicken in hot water and plucked the feathers until it looked more like the kind of chicken I recognized. Much to my surprise, dispatching the chicken wasn't as bad as I'd anticipated.

Later that evening, Sara cooked the chicken—with stuffing and all—and we had a wonderful meal with the guards. If I had been able to suspend belief—just a little bit—it was almost like being at home.

And so we settled in to life in Kenya. The reality was that Sara and I had a comfortable apartment, and enjoyed hot water and electric light, at least most of the time. We managed regular contact with the rest of the world some of the time. Slowly, I began to relax and enjoy everything that was swirling around. On the basis of past excursions abroad, I knew it took me, and those with me, several months to feel comfortable. Having learned to cope with the essentials of daily life in Nairobi, at least from a Western point of view, I was ready to reach out to the friends and colleagues who wanted to help me savor my stay.

A Crazy Quilt

Most cities—in the United States and abroad—contain multiple pockets of different kinds of people. As immigrants from various countries poured into New York City around the turn of the last century, Danish photographer Jacob Riis recorded his impressions of vivid hues in his book *How the Other Half Lives*. "A map of the city, colored to designate nationalities," he wrote in what has become a classic treatment, "would give the whole the appearance of an extraordinary crazy-quilt." Nairobi, Kenya's capital, reminds me of how New York must have seemed to new arrivals a century ago. Within the space of a few short blocks, one community merges into another, and then still another begins. Drive a few miles from the center of town and you encounter even greater contrasts, as wealthy enclaves give way to impoverished slums. Eager to learn as much as I could about my new home, I spent hours walking and driving through different parts of the city.

Like other expatriates, Sara and I both discovered how much we needed friends while living abroad. Travel is an intoxicating elixir, as you move eagerly from one new place to the next. But living in another country is different. Connections count considerably in the effort to feel at home. Sara and I knew the essentials of navigating around Nairobi from previous trips, but soon discovered how much we needed the more important emotional support that only friends could provide.

Fortunately, friends were easy to find, and they came from all over. Nairobi reflects the divisions of the nation at large. Kenya, like most developing countries, is highly stratified, and its major city contains members of all important groups. As the largest urban center in East Africa, it is the economic hub of the region. A prosperous Kenyan elite runs the nation and its members enjoy conspicuous wealth. Kenyans jokingly use their Kiswahili to refer to these people as *wabenzi*—members of the Mercedes-Benz set—in contrast to the *wananchi* or common folk. Nairobi is also home to a multinational business community, and these people, along with their diplomatic and international-development counterparts, mingle with the prosperous African leaders and give the city a multicolored hue. As a wealthy African trader once remarked, "Rich men of all races get on well together." Asians, originally from India, dominate most small businesses—as well as many large ones—and run many of Nairobi's commercial establishments. Brought to Kenya by the British to build a railroad at the end of the nineteenth century, when the British themselves had no intention of providing the labor and the Africans living on the land refused to do such tough manual work for the colonial authorities, the Asians remained in the country and prospered in the years that followed. An African middle class includes small businessmen, government employees, teachers, and artisans. And then there are the laborers, drivers, clerks and others, often unemployed or underemployed, who live in Nairobi's slums.

The geography of the city reflects the social stratification and dates back to colonial days. The wealthiest Europeans, and their African counterparts, live in large houses in a part of the city called Muthaiga. Other whites, both expatriates and people born and raised in Kenya, reside in Karen, a suburb named after Karen Blixen (who wrote as Isak Dinasen), or in other regions such as Lower Kabete, and Langata. Asians still congregate in the area of the city known as Parklands. Squatters and poor African homeowners often live in the Kawangware, Kangemi, and Kibera slums.

Kenya still contains abundant evidence of its colonial past, and once again Nairobi follows the same patterns. The British dominated colonial East Africa. They subjugated the local people and imposed their own system of landholding and law. English missionaries, along with counterparts from other nations, arrived in Kenya in the mid-nineteenth century. Before too long, the British felt fierce pressure to protect the clergy preaching in the region. At the same time, British businessmen began to speculate about the commercial prospects of what they realized was fertile land. Following the opening of the Suez Canal in 1869, Kenya seemed closer to England than it had ever appeared before. In 1896, the British started a massive six-year effort to build a railroad from coastal Mombasa clear across the Rift Valley to Uganda, which politician and statesman Winston Churchill once called the "pearl of Africa." This was an effort to provide access to, and protection for, the source of the Nile. Though it was never a commercial success, the railroad opened Kenya to English settlement and led to the establishment of the city of Nairobi at mile 327 of the railway line. The city's name came from a Maasai word meaning "the place of cold water." Originally little more than a railroad supply depot and switching yard, the community was simply a stopping point in a swamp filled with frogs, where engineers pondered the enormous construction problems that lay ahead. But the temporary settlement took root and, within a few years of its establishment, colonists made it the capital of the entire East African expanse.

Nairobi's most prosperous areas reveal their British influence. The British community is far smaller than it was prior to independence in 1963, but the British who remain in Kenya, some as Kenyan citizens, hold many of the same values as their forebears and help give some sense of what life was like in those earlier years. Many of the settlers in the 1920s and 1930s operated farms in the so-called "white highlands" north and east of Nairobi, but maintained homes in the city as well. There, a mile above sea level, they enjoyed—and still enjoy—the temperate climate near the Ngong hills.

Muthaiga remains one of Nairobi's most prosperous areas. Large houses, including one now inhabited by the American ambassador, line Muthaiga Road. These structures are solid and imposing, many constructed out of stone. Situated back from the street, they all include carefully tended grounds, with bright-flowered flame trees or blue-hued jacaranda trees interspersed with more exotic equatorial plants. Some of the houses look like English country estates. They are seldom close to one another, for the rich can afford room, and often you are not even aware of other homes nearby. Such dwellings obviously require a good deal of maintenance, but (as in colonial days) labor in Africa is cheap.

The Muthaiga Country Club has long been one of the city's most exclusive haunts. Built from large blocks of stone, covered with a pinkish stucco, and punctuated with steel-barred windows, the club catered to the colonial class in the years prior to independence. It was the settlers' headquarters in Nairobi, the place where they organized hunt balls, wild parties, and other well-lubricated revels that were part of the dissolute life style of what came to be called the "Happy Valley" crowd in the highlands. "Are you married, or do you live in Kenya?" was a question often asked as stories of the spouse-swapping escapades of the upper class frequenting the Muthaiga Club made the rounds. Today, as in years past, black African employees take care of the largely white clientele.

Muthaiga is quieter today. The lusty behavior of the settlers of the 1930s is long gone. But this part of the city remains as beautiful as it was before and still houses people who play an important role in Kenya's social and political life. We made friends with a few of the people in Muthaiga. It took us time to learn the language and the customs that would help us build strong friendships with my African colleagues, and some of our first links were to the older, expatriate community. As our circles of friends widened and came to include African counterparts, we continued to maintain ties with older expatriates at the same time.

Robert and Mary were British old-timers, both now deceased, who lived in Kenya for well over fifty years. Robert, when we met him in his nineties, was tall, lanky, and ramrod straight, though he walked with a shuffle that reflected his age. Age, too, had taken its toll on his hearing, and he sometimes sat amiably in the midst of conversations that swirled past him, especially when he turned his hearing aid off. Mary, shorter and hobbled by arthritis, was somewhat younger, heard better, and kept Robert apprised of conversations he may have missed. British by birth, they came to East Africa independently. Robert left England in his twenties, when his family had no money to send him to a university, and took a job with the Standard Bank in Mombasa. Dressed in a wool suit with striped trousers, a bowler hat, and an umbrella, he looked every inch the part of a colonial administrator. After his first wife died in childbirth, he moved to Zanzibar, an island off the coast of neighboring Tanzania, where he headed a branch of the bank. There he met and married Mary, a young teacher who had defied her parents and gone to work in Africa in search of adventure.

Back in Kenya, Robert became president of the Standard Chartered Bank. After retiring in the years following independence, he accepted an offer to head the Kenya Broadcasting Corporation, with responsibility for all radio and television transmission countrywide, eventually turning the position over to a black African colleague.

During the Mau Mau revolt of the early 1950s, in which Kenyans mobilized aggressively in pursuit of independence and the British ruthlessly put them down, Robert was one of those relatively few Englishmen who recognized the need to promote greater racial harmony in the country. He was a close friend of Sir Ernest Vasey, then Minister of Finance, and also chairman of the United Kenya Club. Vasey saw the need for a place where the races could meet, and also saw how important it was to promote the careers of young African executives who would serve as leaders in the country with the inevitable arrival of independence. As he moved to expand and develop the United Kenya Club, he brought Robert in to oversee the financial affairs.

Mary, meanwhile, worked as a home economics teacher. She taught sewing, needlepoint, and a variety of other domestic skills to African girls, and also served as a trustee of a fund that provided scholarships for female students who would otherwise be unable to complete their education.

Robert and Mary represented to me those members of the colonial class who did their best to help build the country with a sense of *noblesse oblige*. Kenya was their home, and while they visited relatives in Britain and other parts of the world from time to time, they always returned to Nairobi.

Robert and Mary lived in the heart of Muthaiga, in a country cottage like that in E. M. Forester's novel *Howards End*. Its stone walls were covered with ivy-like vines, topped with a red tile roof. A hedge of fragrant rosemary plants lined the walk to the front door.

A meal at their home usually began with Robert's favorite drink—a pink gin (gin and bitters on the rocks) that must have dated back to colonial days. Sara and I enjoyed their traditional English fare, roast beef with Yorkshire pudding or lamb chops as a main course, with pie or trifle for dessert.

Robert and Mary were the people who had introduced Sara to the United Kenya Club long before I met her, and so we continued to see them at the UKC. Years ago, some of the white settlers began eating together at one table at these gatherings, and they have continued to meet one another in the same corner ever since.

After eating, we occasionally listened to a speaker, in another carryover from the colonial past. The list of invited speakers is impressive, including Jomo Kenyatta, the freedom fighter and first president, who used the club as his forum when released from detention by the British in 1961. At a time when racial restrictions still limited free expression and Kenyatta was banned from speaking in public, he was able to make a speech at a private club. With reporters listening, he offered a reassuring message "to my African friends." He spoke of his wish to maintain friendship with all Africans, black and white. "Some of you have a notion that Kenyatta is a terrible hater of other people, especially Europeans," he said in that speech. "I am here to tell you that we do not hate anybody." Other speakers at the club, then and now, include ministers, ambassadors, and cultural leaders in a variety of fields from around the world. In the early years, Lady Elizabeth Erskine, a prominent English settler, once observed, "Anyone who had any influence was invited."

Robert and Mary served as my window into white attitudes in Kenya's colonial past. Talking with them, I saw what life was like for Europeans during much of the twentieth century. They were never part of the "Happy Valley" crowd, though they enjoyed the Muthaiga Club, but they were part of the English set that simply assumed the British had the right to prosper wherever the Union Jack, the English flag, was raised. I never failed to enjoy their company, though I sometimes felt guilty at the quiet care provided by the members of their black African staff. I *could* have lived comfortably in colonial days, I sometimes admitted reluctantly to myself, hoping all the while that I would never have let myself get to that point. Sometimes I went outside to talk to the staff—in Kiswahili—perhaps to reassure myself of my own empathy for their way of life, but also to remind myself that life for many Kenyans is vastly different, and far less comfortable, than what Robert and Mary enjoyed.

Kenya has a small American community, and, inevitably, Americans became some of our closest friends. Gloria, now in her early nineties, came to seem like a family member, a friendly aunt who was always there to help or

just provide a cup of hot tea. Sara had met her about fifteen years ago on a
first trip to Kenya, and we have seen her each time we have returned to
Nairobi. Gloria also stayed with us for a week in the United States just after
we got married.

Gloria came to Kenya relatively late, at least compared to Robert and
Mary. Her husband, Gordon, was a journalist who became a United States
Foreign Service Officer and, after a posting in India, where Gloria had wanted
to stay, they had come to Kenya. Gordon served as Public Affairs Officer in
the American Embassy prior to independence, between 1956 and 1958, and
Gloria came to love the country as much as India during that first tour of duty.
Gloria taught school in Kenya, and her experience teaching drew her into the
midst of Kenyan life. When that assignment was over, they went back to
Washington, D.C., but returned four years later in 1962, with Gordon heading the Institute for International Education. They were in Kenya for the
granting of independence the next year.

For all their enthusiasm for the country, they had found some things troubling at the start of their lives in Kenya. At a time when black people were
pushing for equality in the United States, and integration of the schools was
slowly getting underway, they were uncomfortable with the rigid separation
of the races they encountered in colonial Africa. Kenya was like a "mini-
South Africa," as one of their friends later recalled. Gloria was disturbed to
learn that the consul general in Kenya had made arrangements for her daughter to go to the all-white school in Muthaiga. "I thought that was retrogres-
sion," she told us. At an art show, she noticed a group of children of all races
dressed in a common uniform, and asked where they went to school. The
Hospital Hill Primary School, a private institution, she was told. It had been
founded by an Ismaili man and his English wife, when their mixed-race children were not permitted to enroll in white schools. Hospital Hill became the
school for Gloria's daughter, and the place where she herself went to work.

Gloria became part of the life of the country. She watched as Gordon
helped assist an airlift of hundreds of Kenyan students to colleges and universities in the United States in the early 1960s. These students eventually returned to take over the leadership of the newly independent country. Through
her teaching, she became close to the children—black, white, and Asian—of
some of the major figures in Kenya in both the pre- and post-independence
years. Among her friends was Tom Mboya, an outspoken labor leader and
one-time heir apparent to Jomo Kenyatta, until he was assassinated by political enemies in 1969.

Then Gordon became ill with cancer. He and Gloria went to the United
States for treatment, but nothing worked successfully. Gordon died without
ever returning to Kenya. Now Gloria had to decide what to do. Like many

Americans, particularly those with military or diplomatic careers, she had bounced around to a variety of locations. Kenya, her most recent home, was comfortable and affordable, and so she decided to return.

Sara and I saw Gloria regularly during our stay in Kenya. She beamed whenever we knocked on her door. With her own world circumscribed by a progressive hearing loss and an arthritic hip, she welcomed our visits and always had ideas for things we could do together. We, too, kept alert for ways to include her in our plans. Occasionally, I took her to see an American film. When *Forrest Gump* came to Nairobi a year after it opened in the United States, I watched Gloria smile broadly as she became immersed in the cinematic representation of events she and Gordon had lived through together, even as she strained to hear.

Other Americans helped me see another side of Kenya. Ruth, one of Gloria's friends, had her own story. I had just read Barack Obama's book *Dreams from My Father: A Story of Race and Inheritance*, which chronicled his effort to explore his Kenyan roots. Obama, an American who had been president of the *Harvard Law Review* earlier in his life, was the child of a Kenyan father who, while studying in the United States, had married an American woman. Now I learned that Ruth was Barack's stepmother, having married his father when Barack's parents divorced. A tall, vibrant woman from Boston, she had met the elder Obama while he was studying for a graduate degree in economics at Harvard. She knew about the first marriage and the mixed-race son now living with his mother and her parents in Hawaii. Only when she moved to Kenya with her husband did Ruth learn that he also had an "up-country" Kenyan wife and two children from that union whom he had never told her about. According to local custom, Kenyan men could have more than one wife, especially if there had been no church wedding involved, and some Kenyans still follow the practice to this day. It is most common on the Muslim-dominated coast of the Indian Ocean, but still acceptable in other parts of the country. For Ruth, and for me as I listened to the story, it came as something of a shock. But she was determined to make her life in Africa work, and so welcomed the up-country children as her own.

Then, as a reflection of how tightly the social circles are intertwined in Kenya, I learned that Gloria's cook many years ago, when she and Gordon had first come to Nairobi, was none other than Barack Obama's grandfather, and Gordon himself had played a small part in helping Barack's father study in the United States.

Still another white community that took me by surprise was the Nairobi Hebrew Congregation. I had never joined a synagogue in any of my other sojourns abroad, nor had I even known about a temple in Nairobi on past trips. But early in my stay this time, I heard about the group and enquired about it further as soon as I could, perhaps as a way of grounding myself in something familiar as I struggled to cope with strange surroundings.

The Nairobi Hebrew Congregation, I soon learned, consists of approximately 150 families, or a total of about 300 people. It is the only Jewish synagogue in East Africa, with its closest congregational neighbor 2,500 miles away. It includes members of old settler families, arrivals who fled the Holocaust in the 1930s, and now Israelis, who began coming in the post-independence years as members of economic and diplomatic missions. Congregants completed their first synagogue in 1914, then built a larger structure in 1954. The group built a large community center in 1939, and renovated it in 1992. Today, the modest-sized building has a light and airy feel and conveys a sense of simplicity. On either side of the main sanctuary are benches for women, running from front to back, for this is a bastion of Orthodoxy, and women cannot sit with the men.

Members of the Nairobi Hebrew Congregation welcomed me warmly. Before I knew it, I was attending *shabbat* services on Saturday morning far more frequently than I did in the United States. Sara is not Jewish and joked about sitting in the gender-segregated synagogue, but joined me on those Friday nights when we were invited to dinner at a member's home after the service. I sometimes wondered about my participation, even as I felt a sense of comfort as one of a dozen people in the *shul* going through a ritual I had never known while I was growing up in the Reform Jewish tradition. Yet the service became more familiar as time passed, and my participation provided me a connection to my own past.

These English-language communities were a small but important part of my life. Early in my stay, I had told myself that the best way to be sensitive to cultural differences, to learn about them, to avoid any taint of repeating the colonial experience, would be to avoid as much contact as possible with other Americans and other white people. I thought I could gain a more legitimate sense of African life by avoiding people like myself. Cross-cultural experiences are never so simple. Sara and I had each other, but we both also felt the pull of companionship among people who shared some of our background, and could help validate the impressions—and frustrations—that were part of daily life. And so we learned to enjoy the contacts we had with people whose lives were, at least superficially, like our own.

Soon, however, we began to make African friends. I was teaching at the university, and my job introduced me to people who became increasingly close. Macharia, who helped us find a flat when we arrived in the country, soon left for a fellowship year at Boston University, and so we only saw him at the beginning and end of our stay. But in that short time, we went to meetings, ate meals, and drank beer together, and he gave me a much better sense than I had before of just how Kenyan universities worked. I was not always comfortable with the slow pace of the bureaucracy, but it was better to know how to deal with difficult problems than not to know anything at all. And it was reassuring, so far from my own university friends, to be with someone who clearly liked to write and to teach as much as I did.

Our neighbor Mary became our closest Kenyan friend. She was a stocky woman with close-cropped hair, a wide smile and infectious laugh, and dreams of finishing her Ph.D. Because she lived just across the hall, we saw her every day. At first there was a measure of distance, mostly because I needed time to become comfortable in my own way. But Mary found our patterns as puzzling as we found hers. She laughed uncontrollably as she saw me in my running shorts going out for a morning jog. Kenya boasts some of the finest distance runners in the world, but very few of them, apparently, live in Nairobi. Often I was the only one running on the streets or on the paths of the arboretum.

Mary, it seemed to me at first, lived in a world of chaos that often appeared out of control. She had to manage a household of eight or nine people in a two-bedroom apartment the same size as ours. While she had up-country girls from near her family home to assist her, she still had to make sure that the daily shopping, cooking, and cleaning were done, and to see that her two daughters, seven-year-old Joy and ten-year-old Sheila, woke up, got dressed, and went to school. I sometimes encountered her on the landing, still in her bathrobe, trying to figure out what she needed to do next, as I went to work. She was like the friendly but flustered manager of a small boarding house where each resident was going off in a different direction. But she always pulled herself together, got to the university on time, and then embarked on the professional part of her day.

Over time, Mary and the kids began to wander across the hall and come into our flat. Mary stopped by after work to talk, ruminate about everything she had to do, or just share a soft drink or a pot of tea. She loved to talk, about Kenya, about her family, about herself, and we were eager to hear the stories she told as she settled in, even if we were sometimes ready for bed. Like Macharia, she helped me negotiate problems in the university, to figure out whom to see and what to do to finalize my teaching schedule or turn in my grades. Once, as I drove her home from a meeting, I was stopped by a policeman on a what I thought was a fabricated charge. I found it comforting to watch her banter with the over-eager officer, and then tell me later that, if I ever had any other traffic trouble, she had a cousin in the city administration who would take care of it. In light of what I had learned about the police and heard about the prisons in Kenya, this offer came as something of a relief.

Mary was amused by the way we lived. "Your home is too quiet," she often said. There wasn't enough going on. As we moved in and out of Nairobi during vacations, in our quest to see as much of the country as we could, she questioned our relentless need to be on the road. For her, as for most Kenyans, the only legitimate place to travel was up-country, back home. "Why are you always going somewhere else?" she wanted to know. She laughed at our eating habits. As we ate more and more of her meals, both in her flat and in our own, we began to insist that she try some of the food we cooked. The meats and vegetables she found strange, even as she gamely ate everything we offered. The green salads we prepared she called grass.

Joy and Sheila came to our apartment regularly to play with the knick-knacks we had bought on our travels and scattered around. Their reactions to all of the "things" we purchased made me pause and think about the differences in our lives. Like most Americans, Sara and I were accustomed to using appliances in everything we did and relied on a variety of gadgets as a matter of course. On the high-tech end, we had a computer and a fax machine in our apartment. At the same time, we filled the flat with lots of other decorative items. We bought both woodblock and silkscreen prints to take home and, rather than pack them for shipment, we kept them on display. We hung pieces of fabric on the walls, and placed small wood and soapstone carvings in odd corners of the flat. A *bao* set, played on a board with a dozen or so hollowed out pockets and a pile of stones, was particularly popular. All of these pieces gave a homey feel to the place, I thought, even if Mary and the girls wondered why we needed them. And, even as I wondered at our own acquisitiveness, I smiled to myself that they kept coming back to play with these things whenever they could.

Outside the university, Sara and I had another group of friends. Frank and Michi were among the people we saw regularly. Frank was a Kenyan who ran a Kiswahili language school and offered cross-cultural training programs for foreign students and other visitors. When we first arrived, he hoped that he could secure a contract to teach Sara's American students, and even though she chose someone else, he hoped to work with her if she ever led her college's Kenya program again. Partly out of friendship, partly out of a wish to observe another language school in action, she took lessons with Frank and his group of teachers for much of the year. Michi was Frank's wife, a German woman who had come to Kenya to serve with an organization much like the Peace Corps and now worked for a German development agency. Their cross-cultural marriage, with its inevitable strains, gave me a first-hand glimpse at another side of Kenyan life.

Frank had been married before and had two children by that union. Since he had not been married in a church, he felt free to leave his wife without the formality of a divorce. He and Michi were subsequently married—in a church, of course—and he later claimed his two children, now aged eight and six, in the Kenyan pattern where men hold most legal and familial rights.

Sara and I saw Frank and Michi frequently in Nairobi. Occasionally we met at a restaurant specializing in *nyama choma* or roasted meat. Kenyans congregate at these establishments, drinking beer and eating slabs of beef or goat grilled over an open flame. Often we were joined by some of the other language teachers—Maina and Kip most regularly—and together we tore at the meat, and mixed it with a hot pepper relish and *ugali*, a corn meal mush that looks like grits and tastes like paste, and, like everything else at this table, is eaten with your hands. The meat was usually savory, if sometimes tough, but the real pleasure was just sitting and bantering with friends. Because Sara and I were both studying Kiswahili and becoming passably fluent, these friends loved to carry on long conversations in the language at a level we could understand. In part, they were showing us off to one other, as if we were trained animals on display. In part, they were showing us how much further we had to go. Yet it was good practice and good fun, and we usually managed to keep things going for an hour at a time, until the beer began to have a dulling effect and a kind of emotional exhaustion set in.

Beer was an important part of the evening, and one beer followed another even before the first was done. It was assumed that once you began to drink you were there for the long haul. Frank loved these occasions, and, like many Kenyan men, could spend the better part of a day drinking with friends. I often got tired after a few hours but Sara had more staying power. This was a side of Kenya she loved—just sitting around, chatting, laughing, with no particular place to go. I was always more focused on what came next, although Kenya did help me learn to savor a different pace just a bit. Eventually, though, Sara would humor me and agree to move on. I could afford to leave without losing face, for I was a *mzungu*, a white person. But the rest of the Kenyans were expected to keep on going, often until the early hours of the dawn. Michi, usually the only woman besides Sara in the group, occasionally pushed Frank to go home, for she had to get up early to go to work in the morning. Sometimes he complied; sometimes he became irritated. The Kenyan patterns of life and marriage to which Frank and his friends were accustomed could cause conflicts between Frank and Michi.

I saw this kind of interaction most vividly when Frank and Michi invited us to visit their family home in Kisii, the world's capital of soapstone carving. All Kenyans consider their place of birth their real home. They may reside in Nairobi, but they really come from somewhere up-country, and return there as often as they can. Frank and Michi rented a house in the city, but built a home of their own in the family compound, to which they traveled four or five hours at least once a month.

We spent a delightful weekend there with Frank's parents and siblings. His father was a former teacher, who was articulate in English and Kiswahili. One sister had just returned from working as a nurse in Saudi Arabia and was now considering moving to the United States. She had the professional skills to be able to gain entrance if she chose. The youngest sister was staying home to take care of her parents.

At one point during the weekend, Frank disappeared. I later learned that he had gone off to find old school friends and spent several hours drinking beer at a small outdoor bar. At first Michi did not seem concerned, but when he finally returned, I realized that she was upset. For the duration of the weekend, whenever Frank seemed ready to head out, Michi made sure that we all followed him, joining the informal party with his friends, settling in together for another liquid afternoon. Once the ground rules were set, the rest of the visit unfolded more easily.

On another occasion, Kip, one of the other language teachers in Frank's group, took Sara and me off on a special outing of his own. He thought we ought to see the Modern Green, a seedy bar in one of Nairobi's seedier neighborhoods. Downing beer after beer, we got involved in a conversation with a drunken artist trying to sell his work, parried the advances of several prostitutes already at work, and watched the efforts of a number of crippled people, who had either gotten rid of their crutches or, more likely, never had them to begin with as they navigated across the room on the floor. This grim experience brought home the poverty so prevalent in Nairobi—and Kenya—and the ways some people dealt with it.

Justus was another special Kenyan friend. He was a taxicab driver in Nairobi, but he was hardly an ordinary cabbie. He ran a family business, hectic but relatively prosperous, catering to a variety of clients. He helped Sara, and other faculty members from her college, organize all the transportation they needed during their semester-long programs in Kenya. And he became a kind of informal advisor, not merely on logistical arrangements but on Kenyan culture itself. For Justus was a worldy philosopher, a shirt-sleeve sage with opinions on both Kenyan and American politics and on social problems around the world. "Now look," he often began as he launched into a discussion about anything whenever we had time to listen. Justus had a goatee in a country of few beards. He drove an old Mercedes, bought for him by a grateful client years before, now held together in patchwork fashion by his mechanically-oriented sons. Later on, he became something of a medicine man, mixing up an herbal concoction that he advertised on the World Wide Web and claimed could cure anything from cancer to a cough.

Justus had come to Nairobi from Kikuyuland years ago, around the time of independence, and the city was now his real home. His compound, which included homes for his sons and their families, in the typical Kenyan pattern, was in a Nairobi slum. He traveled all over the country, but always on business, taking clients wherever they wanted to go. He was among the few Kenyans we knew without an up-country home.

I visited his compound, about fifteen minutes from downtown, regularly. The main roads were paved, but little else had the benefit of concrete. When the rains came, the place was like a swamp. "Do you have your gumboots on?" Justus asked me the first time he took me there. "It gets muddy." At that point, though, it had not rained in a month, and there was no problem. I was, however, given what I knew of Justus's widespread business activities, surprised at the small shanty in which he lived. Walls, made out of thin boards hammered together in a ramshackle manner, without the benefit of even a yardstick, were covered by makeshift wallpaper made out of uncut aluminum sheets used to manufacture margarine cans. There was no electricity; the main room was dimly lit with two kerosene lamps, but a television, powered by an automobile battery, was on in a corner the entire time I was there.

Over the Christmas holidays, when my children Jenny and David were visiting, Justus invited all of us for dinner in his home. For months, he had been talking about providing us with a real treat. Now he slaughtered a sheep for us all to eat. Goat is the celebratory meal of choice, but a sheep is larger and even more special. Justus was signaling that he and his family were entertaining us in style. We had fresh lamb soup, chunks of meat, Kikuyu sausage —a ground mixture of innards stuffed into intestine casing—and finally what was evidently the best part of all—the head itself. We were a little queasy when the head arrived, worried when we realized we were going to have to eat it, relieved that it had not been cooked quite long enough to tear apart and had to be sent back (and wouldn't be ready) before we had to go. All the while Justus provided us with what he called "kill-me-quick"—a clear liquor known as *chang'aa*, something like moonshine, which we mixed with either orange soda or coke.

For much of the evening, our conversation revolved around the TV. One of the two Kenyan television channels was broadcasting an old Madonna movie, and we watched fascinated at the strange spectacle of small Kenyan children who could barely speak English gazing slack-jawed at this icon of American popular culture in what must have been her first celluloid incarnation. "Is this what things are really like in the United States?" Justus wanted to know. Slowly, haltingly, I tried to explain that this was probably not a fair representation of contemporary American life. As we watched Madonna's tart tongue and brusquely abrasive manner, though, I was not quite sure.

Midway through the year, Justus decided to move away from the plot of land he had rented for ten years and buy a place of his own. He chose land about five minutes away, cleared it himself, and slowly began building a home for his family with other structures for his sons. It was a long, slow process. Money in Kenya is hard to come by for most members of the working class, and so the project proceeded in fits and starts. Whenever a little cash was available, Justus bought the necessary materials and hired workers —often at a wage of just a couple of dollars a day—to mix the concrete, pour the floors, build the walls, and frame the roof. The house itself, built wholly without formal plans, began to rise as the months passed. It was far better conceived and built than Justus's former dwelling, done with a sense of style and good taste. Njoroge, his eldest son, built a house that promised to be as attractive as his father's—until he ran out of money and had to wait, perhaps months or years, for the finishing touches to be applied. Kamau, one of the younger unmarried sons, obligated to live in his own house after his circumcision ceremony during adolescence, put up a small one-room dwelling built out of boards with a couple of friends over the space of a few days.

Little by little, the compound became cluttered. Soon there were a half dozen or more vehicles, in various states of repair, parked by the buildings. An outhouse was part of the scene, as it had been in the former compound, and there was a small fenced-in plot where a dozen dogs lived, ready to bark furiously if any strangers came in. Justus kept goats and sheep and rabbits in the compound as well, some of these animals wandering free, and we soon recognized the need to watch where we stepped at all times.

These friendships were important to Sara and me. They taught us more about Kenya than either of us could have learned on our own and provided us with the practical and the emotional framework we knew we needed.

At the same time, I found that the friendships were different from most of those I had in the United States. I spent much of my time in conversations that involved listening to stories other people told. I was interested in their lives— past and present—and the trials and tribulations they had endured. I wanted to find out how things had occurred in the colonial days, how people had responded to the transition to independence, how others coped with the frustrations we all faced. But frequently I felt that I had become a kind of captive audience. White people who had been in Kenya for some time had a whole different set of concerns than my own, and that was doubly true of our older friends. Black Africans faced problems we sometimes had trouble even imagining as they struggled with both personal and professional difficulties that complicated their daily lives. And so Sara and I found ourselves becoming intertwined in *their* lives, perhaps even more fully than we let them become involved in ours.

Sometimes I heard the same stories time and again. I listened over and over to Mary's tales about life in Meru—her up-country home—and Justus's accounts of the problems he faced in building his house. But, as the year wore on, Sara and I found that we seldom talked much about ourselves. We shared occasional stories about the patterns of our life in the United States, and I told colleagues about some of my experiences working in American universities. Yet we seldom shared our more intimate observations.

Perhaps our reticence was at least in part a result of my own natural reserve. Perhaps it occurred because we instinctively understood that people in Africa—black and white—shared an oral culture in which stories were repeated over and over, while we did not. Perhaps real friendships could not be hurried, as deeper relationships did indeed develop in subsequent years.

Limitations notwithstanding, the friends we made were a source of constant support. They helped us deal with our own everyday frustrations and to understand their problems—and the problems of the country—as we became comfortable in calling Kenya a home.

Teach the Children Well

My first encounter with the University of Nairobi should have alerted me to the difficulties that lay ahead. Finding a university flat had been an anxiety-filled process that just happened to work out well in the end. It became a kind of metaphor for the sometimes insurmountable problems that complicated the Kenyan educational system at every turn and were not always as successfully resolved. For at the University of Nairobi, and at other Kenyan universities, the faculty and staff worked in deteriorating buildings, seldom had sufficient supplies, and faced huge bureaucratic obstacles that complicated their efforts to educate their students. I learned to accept the limitations, as my colleagues did, and in the process came to appreciate the extraordinary value Kenyans attached to education and the tenacity with which dedicated teachers maintained a sense of good cheer and a commitment to their craft when less conscientious faculty members might have given up long ago.

Education is highly prized in East Africa, and throughout the rest of the continent as well. It is usually not free, and parents scrape together the necessary funds to pay school fees for elementary and secondary education, with the awareness that attendance can make a difference in their children's lives. In Kenya, a country with one of the highest birth rates in the world, the average number of children in a family is beginning to drop as parents recognize the need to educate the children they have. They are always scrounging for funds—selling a cow up-country if that seems feasible, sometimes even soliciting money from strangers they meet on the street in Nairobi as a last resort. It is not uncommon for students at all levels to sit out a term if funds are unavailable, but they usually return as soon as they can. This, of course, can extend the time needed to complete the course of study.

Education is absolutely essential for advancement in Africa. Here is where students learn Kiswahili, the national language that unifies a country with dozens of different dialects, and English, the official language that is used in all government offices and is the language of instruction in the schools. Education also prepares pupils for what jobs exist in a dismal labor market. Jobs do not necessarily follow from finishing school, to be sure, but are almost impossible to find if you do not attend.

The schools in Kenya now bear a greater resemblance to American schools than they did before. After decades of following the British educational pattern, with "O" level (ordinary) and "A" level (advanced) examinations at the end of secondary school, the nation several years ago implemented the so-called 8-4-4 system, modeled after the American configuration of elementary, secondary, and higher education. Yet superficial similarities should not disguise the differences between schools in Kenya and the United States.

Students in Kenya work hard. Sheila, our friend Mary's ten-year-old daughter, had homework due every day, far more than I remember doing myself or being done when my own children were in school. She took ten subjects, ranging from English to history to art, with regular examinations in all areas. Each class, it seemed, had a required daily assignment. Often I noticed Sheila studying late at night in her family's flat across the landing, by candlelight if the electricity failed, as I went to bed. She sometimes seemed more like a miniature female version of a Talmudic scholar—or an Abe Lincoln in Illinois—than a carefree kid.

Elementary-school children compete to gain admission to the best secondary schools in Nairobi and elsewhere in the country. Students living far from the city are at a disadvantage, for up-country schools are underfunded and less well-supplied. The luckier ones win scholarships providing them with the support they need to continue. Jeremiah, one of my graduate students in the history department, told me that, when he had failed to win a scholarship to high school the first time through, he had decided to repeat eighth grade, even though he had graduated at the top of his class, to stand a better chance of gaining support the next year. His gamble paid off. Other students are less lucky.

Then, at the end of high school, national examinations determine where applicants will go to college. Only about a quarter of the students taking the exams are offered admission to the public universities, and those admitted have no choice about what they will study or where they will attend. You might hope to study science at the University of Nairobi, only to find yourself assigned to pursue literature at Kenyatta University, just outside of town. Would-be doctors sometimes end up as teachers through no choice of their own. That system, based entirely on national exam scores, creates a measure of discontent, muted only by the sense in Kenyan culture that the young are supposed to do what they are told.

In years past, students admitted to Kenya's public universities had all their expenses paid. About a decade ago, all that changed. The World Bank and the International Monetary Fund, organizations that provide huge loans and grants that sustain Kenyan development, told the country that it could no longer afford the huge expense of providing a free college education to all admitted candidates. Part of the structural-adjustment program that was a precondition to continued support entailed students paying part of the cost on their own.

The figures are miniscule in comparison to the cost of a college education in the United States. With the state still continuing to pay public university tuition, students are required to pay about $800 for each academic year for living expenses. Compared to the $35,000 that many American parents pay for a child's attendance each year at an elite private institution, that amount seems insignificant. But it is probably harder for a Kenyan student, in a country where the average per capita income is but a few hundred dollars, to amass that sum than it is for many American students to raise the full total necessary to attend college for a year. And while private universities cost less than their American counterparts, they are beyond the reach of many middle-class families.

The Kenyan government had just issued the decree requiring student contributions toward university costs when I arrived in the country in the summer of 1995 to teach at the University of Nairobi. The new academic year was scheduled to start in August. In July, Kenyan students took to the streets to protest the costs they said they could not afford. In characteristic fashion, the government responded by calling out the police. Peaceful protest devolved into ferocious confrontation, with a number of students being taken to the hospital with cracked skulls and other injuries. In this, as in most confrontations, the authorities won. But the adverse publicity in the *Nation*, Kenya's most influential newspaper, and other segments of the media persuaded the government to ease discontent by implementing a loan scheme to provide the necessary funds.

There had been some loan plans in the past, but the default rate was inordinately high, some said at a level close to 95 percent. With jobs scarce after completing college, many students could simply not afford to pay back what they had borrowed to go to school. But some kind of political response was necessary, and so top authorities decided to push ahead with the loans.

Yet a nationwide loan scheme took time to plan and implement. Figuring a month to design and another month to execute the new financial arrangements, the government announced that all public universities would be closed until mid-November. As one of my colleagues, far more used to university closures than I, told me with a smile, "You've got a vacation on your hands."

For the next two months, I planned courses, did my own writing, and traveled around the country accompanying Sara and her Earlham College students on their program. Meanwhile, the loan scheme slowly got off the ground, with politics intervening, as is so often the case in Kenyan life. Each student had to return to a home village up-country and submit an application to the local chief. Disbursement of funds likewise came to local banks. That provided local officials with an opportunity both to gain political capital and to handle substantial sums, with whatever advantage to themselves that might result. It also meant that indigent students had to make several trips home, all at their own expense, to take care of the necessary procedures.

In November, around the time of the American Thanksgiving, the universities reopened. Almost immediately, students at Kenyatta University, just outside the center of Nairobi, rioted, claiming that loan payments were being parceled out inefficiently and that the university was charging inflated prices for housing and food. Angered at the outburst, the university closed the campus for the next several months.

In February and March, students at Egerton University, several hours northwest of Nairobi, near Lake Nakuru, followed suit. Armed police entered the campus to quell the uprising. Nine students were injured in the clashes that occurred. The vice-chancellor closed the university and suspended students who had been involved.

We were lucky at the University of Nairobi. There, good advice prevailed. It came largely from Godfrey, a colleague in the history department and a former dean who now held an appointment as Special Student Adviser. Godfrey was one of those committed faculty members who cared deeply about his students, his intellectual scholarship, and the state of education in Kenya as a whole. A man with a slight build and a large smile, he had done his undergraduate work at Makerere University in Kampala, Uganda, long before the University of Nairobi had been established. Then, on his own, he secured admission and a scholarship from the Rockefeller Foundation to the School of Oriental and African Studies at the University of London. He had taught on several occasions at both American and African universities and served as a visiting examiner at universities all over the continent. I was flattered when he gave me a copy of his book on the history of the Kikuyu, which provided me with a better sense of one of Kenya's most influential ethnic groups. Over the course of the year, I found myself going to Godfrey to get things done. He had two telephones on his desk (multiple lines had not yet reached the University of Nairobi) and was willing to pick up the phone at any time to help move things along. With an enthusiastic, high-pitched laugh, whether talking over a beer or a cup of tea, he put me at my ease and helped persuade me that good will and good sense could prevail.

As students returned to the University of Nairobi, Godfrey kept his office door open. Some were having terrible trouble getting the promised loans.

Others were still having a hard time making ends meet. As Godfrey watched other Kenyan universities erupt in violence and then close down, he wanted to avoid a similar scenario at Nairobi. He counseled the vice-chancellor and other authorities to try to meet the students halfway, without overreacting to the pervasive sense of dissatisfaction. Thanks to his efforts, the loan funds were made available with a minimum of fuss. Accommodations for needy students who still could not pay were made when necessary. As conditions improved over the course of the year, students felt they had access to a friendly ear, and that helped mute their discontent.

Godfrey remained cheerful, as he did his best to solve insoluble problems. He was saddened by the difficulties he faced on a daily basis. He worried about "a serious hemorrhage of talent," what was already becoming "a very serious brain drain." And, so, he went out of his way to assist students who often had no other person to whom to turn.

He paid a price for his efforts. Recognized internationally as a first-rate scholar, he now had little time for his own scholarship. "One of the sacrifices that you have to make . . . if you are busy with these . . . extramural activities," he once told me, was that "you really don't have the time for research, so your research suffers, definitely." Even so, he remained committed to his task.

As the university prepared to reopen after its unwelcome closure, I was finally able to settle in. I asked Henry, the chairman of my department, about an office. Most of the senior faculty members were located along the third-floor corridor leading to the departmental office, and I hoped to be situated there. But there seemed to be no space available in that corner of the building, and I was assigned to a small cubbyhole upstairs. I requested a desk, a chair, and a bookcase, and within a couple of days those appeared. With maps I secured from the American Embassy, the office soon began to feel comfortable. The only problem I had was getting the lock to function, but after a few days, I learned how to push and tug and make the key work without breaking it in the process.

Then I sat down at the desk to try to prepare an introductory lecture for my U.S. History survey course. As I've mentioned, I am task-oriented, probably too much so, and like to get things done. Though my Kenyan colleagues seemed more relaxed about the beginning of the term, especially with the late starting date, I had things I wanted to do to feel ready for teaching in an altogether new setting. Conditions were pretty spartan at the start. I had no telephone in my office, and I had been warned about the danger of theft if I brought a computer in, so I picked up a pad of paper and a pencil and began to outline my first class. Soon, I was disturbed by a drip of water. The first droplet landed on my pad. The next fell on my head.

The water leak was my first introduction to the crumbling infrastructure at the University of Nairobi, so typical of the country as a whole. The rainy season had not yet arrived, so there was no water pooling on the roof. Perhaps the leak came from a faulty pipe, or from a bathroom fixture that had fallen into disrepair. No one knew, and no one seemed to know how to find out. Maintenance, I soon discovered, was not the university's strong suit. I could file a request for repair, but unless I was willing to move the paperwork myself through all channels and then wait outside the repair shop early in the morning to sidetrack a workman and take him to the office, I stood little chance.

I knew I was in a poor country in the developing world, and I didn't want to make excessive demands, but an office in which I could work, like those my colleagues had, was a priority to me.

I went back to the chairman. "Henry," I said. "Might there be another office, anywhere, that I could use?" On the main floor, there *was* a vacant office, now piled high with broken furniture. One wall had large water stains from ceiling to floor, but at least the wall was dry. Even if the water had seeped in earlier, it was better than the leak upstairs.

Henry was willing to humor me in this request, as in most other things I asked of him over the course of the year. He wanted me to be comfortable and content and able to do the work I had come to do. Like a number of his colleagues, he had been educated abroad, with a Ph.D. from UCLA, and he had some sense of how to make American academics happy.

Within a day, I was in the new office. Sara went over to Biashara Street, where there are numerous fabric shops, and bought me three *kangas*—colorful pieces of cloth with printed borders, designs, and Swahili phrases that seemed like the messages in Chinese fortune cookies—to hang on the walls and cover the top of the desk. Before too long, a telephone appeared. Several of the windows did not close, but since the Nairobi climate was temperate at all times, that didn't matter. I simply dusted the office more regularly than usual.

Several weeks later, just as I was beginning to feel comfortable in my new surroundings, painters appeared. Henry had evidently decided that the splotched walls needed to be covered with fresh paint, and, by some extraordinary effort, he had managed to get the university to send workmen over to do the job. "Another disruption," I muttered to myself, secretly pleased about the concern for my well-being, flattered at the willingness to clean up the room, but also aware of the other things in the university that weren't getting done as my walls were being painted. I moved my belongings out once more, watched as the painters completed their work, and, when they were finished, rehung my *kangas* on the walls. The paint job looked good for the next six months. Then the rains came and the walls began to sweat, just as they did in our flat. Slowly, water stains began to reappear. But the damage seemed relatively minor, compared to what I had seen before, and before things got much worse, it was time to go.

As I settled into my new office, I watched the students arrive on the campus. The University of Nairobi is a residential campus, where all students admitted must live in the housing provided by the school. The dorms leave much to be desired, though; most look crowded and uncomfortable at best. One complex near our apartment was known to students and faculty members alike as Soweto—after the slum township outside Johannesburg in South Africa—in recognition of the poor quality of the structures there.

Even more of a problem was the fact that there were only 9,000 places for students to live, although 12,000 were enrolled. "Why has the university accepted so many more students than it can handle?" I wondered aloud to one of my colleagues. The answer was rooted in the switch from the British to the American system of education several years before. Apparently, the university simply admitted a final class following the English model and a new class all set to begin in the American 8-4-4 pattern at the same time. It was undoubtedly a political decision, to try to keep all constituent groups happy. But it caused, and still causes, untold difficulty for the students involved. Each term, one class had to sit out the semester at home. This staggered approach slows down the whole process and makes it almost impossible to complete a degree in less than five or six years. And that time is extended even further if the university closes down for other reasons, as was the case when I taught there.

The return of the students meant that my classes had to be scheduled, and that proved to be another bureaucratic nightmare, largely because I had no idea what was going on. I was used to our patterns back home, where a faculty member might voice a preference for what he or she wanted to teach, negotiate with the department to make sure all necessary courses were covered, and then settle on teaching days and times long before a new term was set to begin. In Kenya the year I taught there, the process began about the time the students started to arrive. The first part was easy. All members of the history department sat around a table and chose the courses they wanted to teach. Sometimes, when an unpopular course was up for grabs and no one wanted to teach it, there was an uncomfortable silence. At that point, the junior members usually bowed to pressure and their reluctant offer was accepted. Then came the process of scheduling the classes. The history department was assigned a number of time slots by the central administration, but my colleagues still had considerable flexibility if the times provided seemed unsuitable to their needs. I was finally given two hours one day and a third hour the next day for one course, and ended up breaking the group into smaller discussion sections myself later in the term as a means of trying to get the students to talk.

I quickly learned that the first day listed on the official university calendar bore no connection to when classes would actually begin. Students were still collecting their loan checks and settling in, and none of my colleagues seemed eager to begin teaching until the classrooms were filled. So I waited until early December, just a week or two before Christmas vacation, before I taught my first class.

Teaching was what I had come to Kenya to do, and I was relieved when I could actually start. Like many compulsive academics, I define myself according to my work, and part of that process involves interacting with a class. This is only one segment of my academic life, to be sure, but it is an important part, and the long, unanticipated vacation in a faraway land occasionally left me feeling uneasy. I felt guilty about not doing what I had been sent to do and restless with the time off before I had done anything to deserve it. I wanted to share my sense of American culture, and learn more about Kenyan society at the same time. I love feeling connected to a group when I think I'm lecturing well or leading a particularly good discussion, and I missed watching the individual and collective responses to the material I wanted to cover. I was ready to engage a class in a dialogue, where all members participate by listening to what the others have to offer as well as plunging in with their own comments. I assumed I could recreate these patterns in Kenya, just as I had in other assignments abroad.

I was hardly a novice in teaching non-American students. I had taught Filipinos in my Peace Corps days, then Finnish and Dutch students in subsequent years. I had lectured to still other students in a variety of countries around the world. I thought I understood the cultural conflicts that can complicate the educational process for an American professor in a foreign land. Students in the United States are usually more vocal—at least in the classroom—than their counterparts abroad. At the University of Helsinki, for example, expatriate friends were fond of telling a story revealing the reluctance of Finnish students to challenge the authority of faculty members. One American visitor, so the story went, was lecturing about Abraham Lincoln and the coming of the Civil War, and noted that Lincoln had been born on February 22. A bright Finnish student, who had just completed a report on the subject, knew that this date was wrong. Raising her hand, she said, "Sir, isn't it possible that Lincoln was *also* born on February 12?"

Still, for all my past experience, I was unprepared for the silence that often greeted me in my Kenyan classes. My faculty friends were animated and argumentative, eager and willing to talk about anything at all. I loved the conversations we had, both in formal seminars and in casual gatherings in the Senior Common Room. One session on female circumcision in Meru, near the slopes of Mt. Kenya, was the most animated scholarly discussion I had seen in years. When I delivered guest lectures to public groups, people were willing to challenge ideas I presented, and we sometimes engaged in heated debate. But the classroom was different. Students had been trained by the culture, regardless of their ethnic home, to respect parents, elders, and others in authority. In my first classes, mine was the only voice heard. I wondered if the silence was the result of the class being conducted in English, but then I remembered that these students had been using English in the classroom for the past ten years.

Early in the term, I realized that a necessary first step was to learn my students' names. I had struggled with Finnish names at the University of Helsinki, rolling Riisto or Marjatta off my tongue until I became comfortable with the pronunciation. I had fought with Dutch names, like Elzilien or Joka, which were equally unfamiliar. But I had even more trouble with Kenyan names.

I never received an official class list. Rather, I had to construct one myself, complete with names and identification numbers. When I asked for names, though, most students provided me only with a family name and initials. "What do people call you?" I asked. Silence. Finally, I found out that it was customary to call everyone by a last name. I would have to do it that way. Then I looked out at a class with Kanene, Kimani, Kimeli, and Kirumba sitting in front of me. And close by were Mbasu, Mbugua, Mukaisi, and Mulaa. The names swam around in my head, but I knew I was going to have to master them somehow if I ever hoped to encourage the students to speak.

I decided to do something I had begun to do in the United States—take pictures and use them to learn the names. And so I took our small Pentax camera to class, and asked the students to stand together in groups of three or four while I snapped the shots. I was hardly prepared for what followed. At the next class, I brought the prints in with me and asked the students to write their names on their images, without obscuring the face. They were reluctant to spoil the pictures. Then they wanted copies for themselves. At the end of class, one student came up and asked if my in-laws could bring him a camera like the one I had used when they visited Kenya. Prices in the United States were far lower than in Kenya, and if the camera was carried in by a tourist, my student could avoid a substantial duty payment as well. I finally acceded to the request, hoping that this gesture of goodwill might help me in my campaign to get the students to speak out.

Slowly, I learned the students' names. I became more comfortable using their family names, even if I sounded to myself like a drill sergeant as I called them out. In my own academic career, I have used first names as a matter of course to try to foster a friendlier atmosphere in class. Now I had to back off old patterns in my effort to create whatever spontaneity I could in the classroom.

For the first part of the term, I spent most of my time lecturing. I prefer to encourage an interactive dialogue where everyone can participate, but the students in Kenya knew virtually no American history, and I reasoned they needed some background before they were ready to talk about the issues. From time to time, I circulated a document and tried to get the students to reflect on it aloud. "Read the first paragraph of the Declaration of Independence," I told them. "Tell me what you think Thomas Jefferson was trying to say." Total silence. I tried again. "What human values does he consider most important?" Continued silence. With persistence, I was finally able to elicit the most obvious response—"life, liberty, and the pursuit of happiness"—but I realized I was going to have to find other ways of getting the class to talk.

I tried to relate the story of the American struggle for independence to the Kenyan struggle against British colonialism two centuries later. The students began to perk up. The notion that Great Britain might have been doing the same thing to the American colonies in the eighteenth century that it had done in Kenya in the twentieth century got their attention. I pushed the parallel as far as I could. As we talked about the Townshend duties and other levies, and the outraged American response, I was able to tie that to the hut tax the British imposed on the Kenyans in the early twentieth century in an effort to force them into wage labor to serve their colonial masters.

On another occasion, I was talking about the debate over what to call the first American president after independence had been won. Should he be addressed as "Your Highness" or "Your Excellency," in the manner of reigning European monarchs? Or was a simpler term more acceptable? "Perhaps they should have called him *Mtukufu*," I said, and for the first time all term the class erupted in laughter. *Mtukufu* means "Excellency" in Kiswahili, but came to mean something more like "The Most High" or even "Your Holiness" as applied to Kenya's first president Jomo Kenyatta and later to his successor Daniel arap Moi.

But those moments occurred only rarely. Finally, I decided to break the class up into smaller groups of ten to fifteen students to provide a more manageable forum for discussion. I would lecture once a week, and meet the group in these sections the rest of the time. At the first such session, I made a seating chart to help me master names. I brought photocopies of pictures, graphs, and charts to provide something concrete to talk about. And I told the students that I did not plan to lecture, but to sit quietly while they thought about their responses to questions I asked. Several uncomfortable moments passed, but, in the end, they began to offer first monosyllabic answers to my queries, and finally allowed themselves to speculate even further about what some of these documents really meant. Slowly we began to build a sense of trust. Some classes were better than others, but, by the end of the term, I could count on a basic willingness to participate.

One class in particular delighted me. We were talking about the women's movement in the United States, and, to provide a point of comparison, I asked the students about their own expectations for the role of women in Kenya. Perhaps they were finally beginning to feel safe in the classroom. Perhaps I simply struck a raw nerve. Whatever the reason, they reacted vigorously and vocally to my question and soon launched into a discussion that left me far behind. Much of Kenyan society still remains patriarchal, and women function at a clear disadvantage, at least in Western eyes. But the women in the university were beginning to feel that they were entitled to equal rights, and their feelings became clearer and clearer the longer we talked.

One of the men spoke first. He began to articulate what he wanted in a wife. "I'm looking for someone who can cook and clean and take care of my children," he said, and a number of other men nodded in agreement.

A few of the women began to protest that traditional statement of preference. "Don't you want someone you can talk to, like we do here?" one of them wanted to know.

The young man who had begun the conversation shook his head. "It doesn't matter when you get married," he replied. "A wife should know her place."

The women erupted. They were angrier than I had ever seen them, and they didn't hesitate to make their feelings known.

At that point, I tried to get the discussion to focus on questions of housework, and who did what in their homes. Women clearly played the major role in this area, and, in virtually all families, took care of domestic chores. Then the young man who had spoken first about his expectations for a wife made a surprising admission. "My father does some of the cooking in my home," he said.

I was about to question the inconsistency between what he saw and what he wanted when several women in the class beat me to the punch. They were bothered by the almost naive irrationality that threatened to perpetuate patterns they were struggling with themselves. "How can you be so stupid," one yelled. "Why aren't you willing to do some of the work yourself, like your father, when *you* get married?" One after another jumped into the discussion and pounded verbally on their hapless male colleague. I kept quiet, fascinated at the passion that told me so much about tensions in Kenyan society today.

I never had another class quite like that one. I tried to recreate similar preconditions for discussion, but the students failed to respond in the same way.

That session on gender roles did promote a greater willingness to talk for the rest of the term, though never with the same heartfelt intensity about an issue that was so much a part of their lives.

Graduate students were different. They had successfully served an undergraduate apprenticeship, and now had a status that entitled them to speak out more openly. The graduate program, in history at least, was also tiny, and the students who enrolled were part of a self-selected group. The year I taught at the University of Nairobi, there was just one fellowship available for a new student, and that meant that Jeremiah was the only first-year participant in the program. Rather than take a series of small seminars with other students, as he would have done in a larger program, he worked on an individual basis with me and the other instructors guiding his studies.

Jeremiah had struggled throughout his academic career to find the money to continue school. Now he had support for graduate study, and he intended to make the most of his chance. He was a short, slight, intense man in his late twenties who looked about ten years younger and took his work very seriously. Like most Kenyan students, he was polite with teachers and others in authority, sometimes to the point of subservience at first. But he was also willing to carry on a discussion, with both questions and comments of his own about the issues we were considering in our tutorial sessions.

At first Jeremiah came to our meetings having done the textbook reading assigned, with questions he wanted to ask. Our sessions frequently involved working our way through his lengthy list of queries, as I tried to respond by providing background he needed to know. As time passed, however, I began to ask the questions, and to push him to respond to issues I felt were important. Though he resisted at first, by the end of the semester we achieved the give and take that produced thoughtful conversations about the patterns of the American past.

Though English was not Jeremiah's native language, he spoke and wrote well. I realized how bright he was when I read the first paper he handed in. It was a thoughtful assessment of the causes of the American Civil War that showed an ability to organize material and to think conceptually about the larger topic of historical causation. Jeremiah had clearly considered the issues and developed his own interpretive framework. I read through the essay, correcting grammar, polishing prose, and questioning a number of his arguments. I then asked him to rewrite the paper, as a way of further improving his use of the written word. He responded to my criticisms and made the necessary corrections. But on issues about which he felt strongly, he refused to back down. I was pleased to see that kind of intellectual tenacity, as he struggled to master this field and to make it his own. Such determination had helped him survive in the past and would stand him in good stead in the rest of his academic career. I was delighted when he later won a graduate fellowship to Miami University—my own home institution—to continue his education in the United States.

Jeremiah and my other students faced difficulties that would have made American students blanch. The library was perhaps the worst of their problems. Early in my stay, I realized there were no adequate textbooks, at least not in my field, and I arranged to have copies of a book I had helped write be sent over from the United States. The dozen copies I put on reserve in the library served the fifty students in one class, and we got through the term reasonably well. In the second semester, I was able to secure at cost outdated copies of another paperback text I had co-authored, and I passed these on to the students for what I had paid. They were pleased to have copies of their own at a price they could afford.

But Jeremiah was a graduate student and needed something more. At first, I told him to go over to the main library, a large, well-designed building with a clean, white stone facade in the center of the University of Nairobi campus. From the outside, it looked like a good library, and I was sure he could find at least some of the titles I suggested. Week after week, he came back unable to locate the books I had recommended. Finally, I went over to the library myself. Some of the titles were in the card catalogue on the first floor but were nowhere to be found on the shelves. When I asked a circulation librarian if missing books could be searched for, she just laughed.

The stacks were a mess. Books that needed reshelving were piled randomly in corners where they remained untouched for weeks and months at a time. The shelves were disorganized, and call numbers bore little or no relation to where the books should have been housed. The whole situation made me sick. I grew up with a sense of appreciation for books and libraries, and I love to browse in the stacks and read whatever I find. No wonder Jeremiah had so much trouble. I finally resorted to the expedient of wandering through the stacks myself, looking at titles wherever books happened to have been placed, picking up things I thought he ought to read. It was a haphazard way of proceeding, I knew. But it was all I could do.

From prior trips to Africa with Sara, who is a professional librarian, I knew that Kenyans always needed books, and I was determined to contribute what I could. Before I left the United States, I had cleaned out my own office, and with those books and other volumes from colleagues and friends, I had assembled a collection of twenty-eight boxes to ship overseas. Support from the United States Information Agency helped cover the cost of transit, and I looked forward to the arrival of the boxes in Kenya during my stay.

As I grew increasingly frustrated with the state of the library, I became worried about the fate of those books. I had no word at all for six months, far

longer than the sea voyage should have taken, even on a ship sailing around
the Cape of Good Hope. Finally, the American Embassy traced the boxes to
the corruption-riddled port of Mombasa, where they had been sitting for most
of our stay. Perhaps they had been misplaced by a low-level employee uncertain where they should go. Perhaps customs inspectors were waiting for a
bribe. I never knew and considered myself fortunate simply to have found
that the boxes were still there. Once they had located the elusive shipment,
embassy officials were able to extricate the boxes from the port, without paying any bribe that I knew about, and now I had to decide where they might
go.

Initially, I had thought I would simply donate the books to the University
of Nairobi library. After my experience with finding reading material for
Jeremiah, I began to think that this would be like dropping them into a bot-
tomless pit. But there was an alternative. The history department had a small
departmental library housed in a single room next to the office. It was a mess.
It contained a reasonable collection of European titles, some books in American history, and random volumes dealing with a wide variety of other subjects. It also had an old, semifunctional mimeograph machine, a broken type-
writer, and a collection of examination papers and exams from the past
twenty years, in no particular order, sitting in pools of mimeograph ink on the
floor.

The room seemed to have real possibilities. I asked Henry, the chairman, if
I might clean it up, rearrange the collection, and add the twenty-eight boxes
of books. He was delighted, and contributed the three hundred dollars necessary to build additional shelves along the walls.

Although I was learning to change my expectations, I still assumed that the
shelves could be built quickly and that Sara and I could get down to the work
of reorganizing the room. But week after week passed and nothing got done.
When I asked Henry if there was a problem, I learned that the request for the
history department to spend its own money on this modest improvement had
to work its way up through every level of the university bureaucracy, and
there was apparently no way to expedite the process.

After a few months, Henry was elected Dean, and in that position he had a
little more leverage. He was now able to pinpoint the progress of our request,
and to encourage subsequent officials to pass it along. Finally, just two weeks
before Sara and I were to leave Nairobi, he told me triumphantly that everything was approved.

The only thing left to do was to get the money from the bursar. I went to
the appropriate office. I was told to return the next day. Then the next. On the
third day, I went to the bursar's office in the morning, and this time I got to
speak to the bursar himself. He told me to come back that afternoon. When I

returned once more, the money was still unavailable. By this time, the mild-mannered, even-tempered, courteous departmental secretary was with me, and she was beginning to seethe. Finally, I told the bursar's secretary, as politely as I could, that I was leaving, and that I was returning the books to the American Embassy, with a special letter to the vice chancellor telling him why this was being done. That threat must have made a difference. The bursar stormed out of his office, muttered in fury and frustration at me in Kiswahili words that even I understood, and handed me the papers to take to another window to get the cash.

The shelves got built in time. Friends in the department moved all of the junk out of the room. The son of a friend of ours helped me unload the boxes, and Sara and I spent several days organizing the books on the shelves. As we prepared to leave Nairobi and return to the United States, we knew that students in at least some fields would have easier access than Jeremiah to books they could use in their academic work.

The entire episode was a kind of microcosmic study of the problems of trying to get things done in a developing country. This was a minor, almost inconsequential project, but it was similar in everything but scale to rebuilding the highway to the coast or refurbishing the international airport. The bureaucracy was almost impenetrable, dominated by officials afraid to take the initiative, for fear of committing too much, accomplishing too little, and losing their jobs. And so small tasks that should have been quickly done either took forever or never got done at all.

To be honest, I was usually the only one upset by delays. Kenyans took things in stride, and knew better than to get irritated by such difficulties. Over the course of the year, I came to recognize the value of a more relaxed approach, in principle at least, even as I recognized that I would probably never be able to let things glide by me in the same way.

And I knew well that my difficulties at the University of Nairobi paled against those faced by permanent members of the faculty. My colleagues had a sense of purpose and professional pride. They were eager to pursue their own scholarship and to teach as well as they could. Yet they worked under conditions that would have appalled their counterparts in the United States. Lecturers at the University of Nairobi—young faculty members, often without doctoral degrees, who do a large part of the teaching—were paid approximately $100 a month and received housing and medical care. Full professors earned a little more, perhaps as much as $150 a month, and likewise got housing and medical care. But Nairobi is not a primitive backwater where the living is cheap. Automobiles, ubiquitous in the city, cost as much as they do in America. Computer prices, in U.S. dollars, are slightly higher than in the United States; as a percentage of a person's income, they are significantly greater. Faculty members found it difficult to pay for groceries for a sizable family out of their monthly salary. "Even buying a shirt becomes a family decision," a senior lecturer in law once remarked.

Most faculty members I knew, even those in administrative positions, taught additional classes on the side at other institutions. Moonlighting was a way of life, and so professors headed for United States International University, which has a campus in Nairobi. It catered to older students who attend evening classes while holding down daytime jobs and others whose scores on entrance exams may not have qualified them for admission to the government-supported national universities. This university hired many part-time instructors and paid them three or four times what Kenyan universities paid their full-time professors. This was the only way many academics could survive.

Most faculty friends found it equally difficult to pursue their scholarship. Very few academic journals are published in Kenya, and journals and publishing houses in other African countries are just as scarce. Europe and the United States offer publishing opportunities for African scholars, but it costs a good deal to mail submissions abroad because postage rates are high. While I was in Kenya, I read a manuscript for a scholar at the University of Benin in Nigeria. When I mailed it back to him from Kenya, it cost me $35, which would have been a prohibitive amount for an academic earning only $100 a month. Travel budgets are likewise limited, and unless conference sponsors provide funds for Kenyan participants, it is difficult to go.

Most of my friends on the faculty were frustrated with the conditions they faced, and disturbed by the administrative structure that located all authority in the national universities in the Office of the President. Because Moi was chancellor of all public universities, political priorities, rather than academic values, prevailed in the decision-making process. Professors, who once had greater stature in Kenyan society, now found themselves falling behind, both by material and non-material measures. Godfrey spoke for most of them in recalling better days, when faculty members "were recognized as being important personages in this country."

Several years ago, more aggressive academics sought to form the Universities Academic Staff Union. They were encouraged by the advent of multi-party democracy in 1992, and hoped it might hail the advent of liberalization in other areas of Kenyan life. They applied for official registration from the government's Registrar of Societies, which is necessary before any meetings can be legally held. A year later, the government had still not responded, and the union leaders called a national strike. They were joined by most of the nation's 3,700 faculty members, and their strike lasted for nine months.

The government responded brutally, as it did whenever it felt threatened. President Moi declared the union illegal. Armed police entered Kenya's college campuses and broke up meetings of union leaders and students. They erected temporary police posts on the campuses to intimidate the strikers and their supporters. They arrested the leaders, including union head Korwa Adar. It was a political struggle, and, as Adar noted, the government won. "The bottom line is that they'll sacrifice anything, even the universities, to keep their hold on power," he observed ruefully. In September 1994, most academics, in dire need of money, went back to work. The union leaders, Adar among them, were fired from their jobs and evicted from their homes. The government swore they would never be hired again—ever. When I was in Kenya, protest had died down. Adar was still embroiled in legal difficulties. He remained upbeat, but finally had to leave the country to find a job. Others were more despondent. "Nobody dares make a noise now," one lecturer said. "There's been a silent death of the universities."

Students were similarly at loose ends. Their protests over increased costs brought a favorable response, but in the following year, after we had gone, the government made it clear that it would tolerate only so much dissent. In mid-December 1996, police shot and killed two students at Kenyatta University who were protesting the death of an Egerton University student at the hands of police the day before. The Egerton student had been part of a larger protest over a refund of $9.89 students said the university owed each of them. Then, in February 1997, a bomb exploded in the room of Simon Muruli, killing the third-year student at the Kikuyu campus of the University of Nairobi. He had earlier complained publicly about dismal university conditions and had told fellow students about death threats he had received in response to his complaints. He claimed, too, that he had been harassed by the police.

After Muruli's death, Nairobi students took to the streets. First hundreds, then thousands of students joined the protest. Mourning their fellow student, they erected barricades and began stoning vehicles. As diplomats from the United States and other countries expressed outrage at the killing, which they called "violent and so far unexplained," and called for a prompt investigation, the vice chancellor closed the University of Nairobi indefinitely. A month or so later, the university was back in session, but then, in mid-April, another policeman killed another student at the University of Nairobi, on the suspicion he was a robber. Friends told me the institution was like a kettle coming to a boil.

Violence erupted again in the summer of 1997. Old grievances remained unaddressed, and now students joined a more general call for greater democratization in political affairs. When I was back in Nairobi that summer, I watched students charge the police in a series of pitched battles that ended up leaving many of them injured and some dead. On a another trip to Kenya in 2003, Egerton University faced further student challenges as it tried to maintain its own stability.

For all of the disruptions, I found the University of Nairobi a hospitable place. My colleagues made me feel at home, and welcomed me as a friend and associate in a common cause. They shared their frustrations, but without the kind of bitterness that might have been expected. Godfrey served as a kind of model, both for me and my colleagues. He retained his sense of humor and his sense of hope that conditions would improve. He had been offered powerful positions in Kenya and prestigious posts around the world, but chose to remain at the University of Nairobi. "In my own opinion and conviction, I don't think I should run away because this university is facing problems," he told me. "I think I would rather be part and parcel of trying to look for solutions to those problems. I do not want to abandon the ship because it is adrift. So, quite frankly, I'm hopeful that the situation will get better."

My students, too, made my experience worthwhile. They broke through their silence at last and, by the end of the year, felt more comfortable asking me about my own life and career as some of them began to dream about the possibility of studying abroad. In subsequent years, I was able to help arrange for several of them to gain fellowships in the United States and to work toward graduate degrees there. Meanwhile, most of them—and their mentors— managed to continue, with good humor, in the face of problems we would have considered intolerable in America. But then I would meet with some of those in the forefront of the continuing struggle for better conditions and remember that the steam could blow things sky high if the simmering water in the kettle ever came to a full boil.

The Realities of Race

When I was in college at Harvard in the mid-1960s, several African-Ameri-can friends spoke occasionally about the awkwardness of being the only black person in a seminar or a dorm. No matter what they did, they told me, they stood out. They were always conscious of that difference and knew that their white friends were conscious of it as well. Even if white classmates were open and accommodating, as most were, the awkwardness still took time to overcome. My friends' perception—and inevitable discomfort—took me by surprise, for I had never really thought much about racial differences before. Like many white Americans, I was largely insulated from such issues in the homogeneous community where I was raised, although my parents talked to my sister and me about the important efforts of the early civil rights move-ment in the 1950s. In subsequent years, as the civil rights movement un-folded, the question of race became impossible for me, and for everyone else, to ignore. My father marched in a protest demonstration in Selma, Alabama, in 1965. Later still, as I became an American historian, I began to study racial conflict and the legacy of discrimination that continues to this day. Even so, as I began to live in Kenya, I found myself acutely conscious of color all the time. If I walked down the street alone, I noticed that I was usually the only white person on the block. If I went into the outdoor market in Nairobi, I needed to steel myself to ignore the cries of *mzungu*, the Kiswahili term for European now used to refer to all whites. I was, without question, a member of a distinct minority, just as my black friends at Harvard had been years be-fore, and for me, as for them, it was something I had to learn to accept.

My parents had had a few African American friends when I was a small child, and I can remember visiting them in their homes and welcoming them into ours. But most of my elementary-school classmates had been white and

few of us had ever questioned why that was so. Later, when my family moved
from a Rutgers University faculty-housing complex to the nearby suburban
community of Highland Park, New Jersey, there were more black faces, but
the number still remained small. The college-preparatory classes I took had
no African Americans in them at all, as my school, like most in the 1950s,
prided itself on the informal tracking system that channeled the so-called
gifted, or socially and economically privileged, students toward professional
careers and left the others far behind. The black students I knew were on the
football and basketball teams, where I watched them play, and on the track
team, where we competed together.

Harvard was different. The university responded to the *Brown* v. *Board of
Education* decision of 1954 and the Montgomery bus boycott of 1955 by
seeking to create a larger black student pool. Henry and Charlie, two of my
friends, were beneficiaries of that move. Both came from middle-class families, one from Washington, D.C., and one from Detroit, and both had been
among the first black scholarship students recruited to the Phillips Andover
Academy, one of the nation's best, and most exclusive, private boarding
schools. Harvard was the next—and the most logical—step.

Living with Henry and Charlie my senior year was one of the best parts of
my college career. Other black students came by our suite, and I listened to
their easy banter in a kind of coded vocabulary that was different from what
I usually heard. "Hey, dude," Paul said whenever he came in. "What's hap-
penin', man?" American popular culture had not yet made that expression
commonplace, and it was certainly new to me. I watched with interest as
Charlie spoke one way to me and our other white roommates and another way
to his black friends. This was similar, of course, to the different postures my
Jewish immigrant grandfather struck with members of his *shul* and people in
the gentile community with whom he worked, but it was still my first glimpse
at a larger black world.

There were other highlights during the year. At one point, Henry and I traveled to the Midwest to look at graduate schools. We stayed with family and
friends, my first excursion into black communities in Cleveland and Chicago.
I sat for hours at a stretch listening to conversations that swirled around me,
recapturing the adventures of relatives and friends. It was, I suspect, much
more exciting for me to stay with Henry's elderly black aunt, or the mother
of a friend, than it was for Henry to stretch out on the cluttered floor of my
cousin's apartment in Ann Arbor.

I became even more aware of racial differences as I began to travel abroad.
Every day, as I walked through the streets of Ormoc City, Leyte, in the Philip-
pines, during my Peace Corps service, little children followed me, yelling,
"Hey, Joe, Give me money Joe." Joe, of course, was G.I. Joe, the American

soldier who had liberated the Philippines from Japanese rule and so started the process that culminated in independence as the war came to an end. G.I. Joe was a hero, and I suppose I should have been flattered by the designation. But the children who followed me were too small to remember the end of the war twenty years before, and most of them could not even speak English. They had picked up the "Hey, Joe" refrain from older siblings, or from an older generation, and now echoed those words only because I looked different from all of the other people on the street.

The "Hey, Joe" refrain reverberated twenty-five years later when I came to Kenya, only this time I was called by a different name. Because of the patterns of African colonization, *mzungu* defined me as a lighter-skinned denizen of a distant land. I had been called a *haoli* in Hawaii, and a *gaijin* in Japan, with both terms meaning a foreigner, noticeably different from the local people. *Mzungu* was somewhat different. I was not simply from a different part of the world, but was of different stock. More than in Hawaii or Japan, it seemed to me, my color was what was being singled out for attention, and sometimes, I felt, for derision.

At first I was bothered by the term and the attention. I found it irritating to be followed by little children, fingers jabbing at me, shouting out a chorus of "*Mzungu, mzungu, mzungu.*" I resented being designated as different, even though the difference was obvious and unavoidable. In Kenya, and particularly in a rural village, I was an oddity, even an object of entertainment, and might be talked about for the rest of the day. After years of being able to blend into the background, in classes, or assemblies, or crowds, I now stood out, much like Henry and Charlie in my college days, and I found there was nothing at all I could do to change the framework by which I was defined.

Slowly I came to realize that the term itself, *mzungu*, was different from other racial epithets. It defined me as dissimilar, to be sure, but in a descriptive way. I was part of that group of outsiders who had come to Kenya, and the rest of Africa, seized the land from people who had lived on it for centuries, and imposed their values and mechanisms of control on those who were not strong enough, or organized enough, to resist. It was not a designation I appreciated, but I had to admit it was true. And even though colonialism was gone, the legacy lingered on. Black Africans controlled the country, but white businessmen and traders from around the world still exercised enormous influence and stayed in the best hotels and most exclusive parts of town. Whether I had such resources myself was irrelevant. I was, by virtue of my color alone, a member of that group.

At the same time, *mzungu*, I came to realize, lacked the demeaning implication of "nigger" in our own country. It didn't marginalize me, and wasn't aimed at undermining whatever dignity I had. I disliked the term *mzungu*, and cringed whenever I heard it applied to me, but still had to acknowledge that it was not really meant to strip away my humanity or my sense of myself.

Still, I resisted the all-too-easy categorization whenever I could. Much of the time I lived in Africa, I tried to distance myself from the whites I saw walking in the streets, as if to persuade myself, naively and erroneously, that I was not really a *mzungu* at all. I felt something like my contemporaries in the Peace Corps thirty years before. Living in Southeast Asia at the height of the Vietnam War, we tried to separate ourselves from the soldiers and diplomats and bureaucrats who were prosecuting the war. We were different, we said. We weren't like those other people who had brought on the war. Now I tried to do the same thing in Kenya whenever I heard the word *mzungu* cast my way. Sometimes I responded with a comment in Kiswahili, as if to say that I wasn't really a *mzungu* at all. But using language to try to soften what I felt was a derogatory term didn't help. Neighbors and friends accepted me as I was. For the little kids on the street, I was a *mzungu* now and forever, and that designation would never change.

Sometimes, the taunts became more pointed. Once as I was walking along Kenyatta Avenue, one of the main thoroughfares in Nairobi, I was suddenly accosted by an African in his thirties who said, "How are you?" in that curious Kenyan lilt, with the intonation rising at the end of the phrase. I had expected to hear the Kenyan equivalent, *"Habari yako?"* and, without thinking, muttered *"Nzuri"*—Fine—in response as I walked away. But my answer was clearly not enough for him. As I continued to move on, I remembered Sara telling me about a similar confrontation she had had with the same man on the same corner just a few days before. This man was eager to engage whomever he could in conversation, and had his own agenda in mind. The man persisted, asking in English, "What's the matter, don't you like to speak to Africans?"

Responding in Kiswahili, I sought to be as polite as I could. I moved along briskly and tried to get by, now that I knew what was coming, but he refused to let me go. Falling in step beside me, he asked, "Don't you like black people?" And then he added, "I know all about America and what you do to black people in the United States." It was not so much a political statement, I realized, as a creative scam: he was playing on race, and racial stereotypes, and the sins of colonialism, in an effort to provoke a sense of guilt, and then recompense. And I, feeling guilty despite my irritation, shrugged, as Sara had told me she had done, determined now not to engage him at all. But my brusque response only irritated him and encouraged him to press on. He repeated his questions, more forcefully each time, so now people were looking at us as we passed them on the street. I was afraid I might be singled out by an angry crowd for having done something wrong, and I was fearful of the kind of vigilante justice I sometimes read about in the local press, a vigilantism that I knew was buried in the American past as well. I began to walk as fast as I could, in an effort to escape before the situation got out of hand.

As the man finally let me go, perhaps to wait for another vulnerable *mzungu*, I couldn't help thinking about what he had said. I was disturbed about being accosted on the street, though I had not been manhandled or physically abused, but was even more troubled by the crass way he had played on my own racial sensibilities. I *was* conscious almost all the time of being white in a black land. Yet there *were* moments when I walked through town completely oblivious to color. Then a quick encounter with a street child or a beggar or even a store owner who looked at me with a kind of hungry interest reminded me that the difference was still there. I had a large circle of close black African friends throughout Kenya and even more black African acquaintances among the students and colleagues who accepted me on my own terms and made me feel comfortable, so much so that issues of race often seemed to disappear. Yet, whenever I ventured out into the larger community, I felt the sense of difference reappear. There was, I often felt, no place to hide. And I resented it, while I also understood it.

Occasionally, the racial confrontations proved more troublesome than that confrontation on the street. I was terrified whenever I was singled out by the police. Police checks are a way of life in Kenya, and barriers frequently bring traffic to a halt, as police officers examine all trucks and buses and cars for possible violations in a transparent play for the payoffs that move the vehicles along. Sometimes the police waved me down in Nairobi, just to check that my license and car registration were up to date. I knew that my black African friends were often stopped as well, and sometimes apprehended if they failed to pay a bribe. They were equally irritated with the situation, especially if they had to spend either time or money to extricate themselves from this fabricated mess. But I was even more fearful, for I was a both a foreigner and a vulnerable white face and could never escape the assumption still reverberating throughout Kenya that I was a member of the once rich and powerful colonial class. My worst nightmare in Africa was of being arrested for imagined transgressions and trapped in a filthy, crowded, rat-infested Kenyan jail, where my white skin would not only fail to extricate me from the mess but might cause even further problems. In my troubling fantasies, I wondered to myself if my whiteness was a kind of inverted mark of Cain—the justification once invoked for enslaving black people—and if I would be made to pay for what other whites had done in centuries past. My fantasies of jail were mostly that; in a country that relies heavily on tourism, white people are not often made targets by the police. But I *felt* vulnerable, and that was something I couldn't escape.

Such confrontations forced me to reflect on the long history of racial tension that was part of the colonial period in Kenya. Rigid patterns of racial discrimination had predominated throughout colonial rule. It was inevitable that I, an outsider, would be linked with the racial repression that had left all Africans of color at a disadvantage when dealing with the imperialists who imposed control. In the United States, South Africa has gotten most of the press over the years for its brutal and inhumane apartheid regime. But the patterns were not drastically different in a number of other countries, and Kenya was among those where a rigid separation of the races was the norm.

Nairobi was a divided city from the time it was founded. White people lived in what residents still euphemistically call the "low density" areas of large estates and manor houses. Asians—mostly Indians—lived primarily in "medium density" regions, where middle-class houses were closer together, though, as some businessmen prospered, they built larger dwellings in these parts of the city. And finally there were the "high density" areas, which included the ramshackle slums occupied by black Kenyans.

Those residential divisions, originating in the past but still visible today, tell only a part of the story. The rigid residential patterns of years past reflected even sharper patterns of separation that governed peoples' daily lives in the colonial years. During my year-long stay in Kenya, I spoke to Charles Njonjo, a once-powerful politician relegated to private life. Njonjo's father, recognizing the value of education, had sent his son to Great Britain, where he attended London University and the London School of Economics and was admitted to the English equivalent of the bar. He returned to Kenya in 1961, on the eve of independence, and found himself in an awkward position. Though he was well-trained as a British barrister and superbly qualified for a prominent post, he was not sure what opportunities were available under British rule. Indeed, as historian Basil Davidson, writing about the entire African colonial experience, has noted of those making the effort to get such training: "It did them no good. The more they proved they knew, and the more artfully they argued their case for admission to equality of status, the less they were listened to. Better by far, pestered officials were bound to think, the 'uncorrupted child of nature' than these wretchedly 'Europeanized Negroes.'" At the same time, Njonjo had to deal with the restrictive racial customs that prevailed prior to independence. "There was no place where you and I could go," he told me as he recalled the colonial days, for he was black and I was white, and virtually all restaurants and hotels had maintained the rigid pattern of separation that the British had established in preceding years. Black people served whites as maids, waiters, laborers, and guards, but that was the extent of the contact.

Others of various colors to whom I spoke recalled similar complications in their lives. Joan, an English woman, came to Kenya in 1946, having recently married an Indian named John, who belonged to the Ismaili sect led by the spiritual leader the Aga Khan. Indians were treated as badly as black Africans in Kenya in those days. They suffered the dual indignity of being darker-skinned than the whites and of being viewed as greedy and grasping entrepreneurs eager to fleece their less fortunate customers. Many businessmen found themselves fair game for jealous attacks that sought to undermine their commercial advantage. Joan's family had even further problems, she later recalled, for theirs was "almost the first mixed marriage in that mini-South Africa, which Kenya was in those days." Racism "permeated the whole of life in Kenya at the time," she continued, and "every aspect of life in Kenya was racially segregated. This included education, sports bodies, hospitals, hotels, etc. John and I could not eat in the same restaurant, and he could not, for instance, join the MacMillan Library, as non-whites could not be trusted to care for books!"

Racial lines became even more rigid in the early 1950s, in the Mau Mau conflict against the British. Freedom fighters, most of them Kikuyus, swore a blood oath—cutting themselves and mingling their blood to seal the pact—to oust the English colonists from the White Highlands where colonial masters had expropriated most of the land. They began a concerted, and effective, guerrilla campaign. The British responded by imposing a state of emergency, passing a series of laws outlawing resistance in any form, and mobilizing troops to quell the revolt. In the process, relations between blacks and whites became even more tense. Though far more native Kenyans than Englishmen were killed in the uprising, the British feared the prospect of continuing racial violence, and wondered how long they could survive in such a highly charged state. For the most observant, independence was inevitable.

With the granting of full autonomy in 1963, Kenyans assumed control of the government and the apparatus that had been used to keep them in check. Jomo Kenyatta became the first president, presiding over a largely black bureaucracy, even as he counseled the need for racial healing and assured whites that he didn't intend to drive them away. As black Africans seized opportunities that had been closed to them for so long, Kenyans, like citizens of other newly independent nations, still carried with them the corrosive effects of colonial rule.

The legacy still exists today. It can lead unscrupulous business leaders and politicians to recreate the patterns of the past and pursue personal advantage, as the British had, and it thus contributes to the ubiquitous corruption that pervades most of Kenya. It also prompts the assumption that all white people have substantial amounts of money that should be shared among those with less in Kenya. I often found it hard to walk down the street in Nairobi without being approached by children collecting money for a church or school or to pay school fees. These were not street children or beggars, rag-covered urchins who lived in abject poverty with no prospect of improvement. Most were middle-class students, often decently dressed, who were hardly scrounging for the next meal but rather for a chance to get ahead. Jomo Kenyatta had pioneered the *harambee*, in which everyone pulled together for a common end, and it has become a national institution, used to raise money for various causes all over Kenya. It is almost impossible to escape at least some kind of solicitation every day. Sometimes I gave a few shillings to an eager student if I was comfortable with the cause. On other occasions, I put my head down, avoided eye contact, and proceeded on my way, nonetheless feeling guilty at my own unwillingness to respond more openly to such demands.

Asians today remain as vulnerable as they were in the past. President Daniel arap Moi courted the Asian community and relied on it for financial help, in return for protection that maintained the delicately balanced status quo. But Asians know that upheaval is possible at any time. They need only to look at neighboring Uganda, where just several decades ago the ruthless dictator Idi Amin slaughtered tens of thousands of their counterparts and drove the rest from the nation. The disquiet in Kenya's Asian community was compounded a few years ago when opposition politician Kenneth Matiba played the racial card, in a bald bid for electoral support, by proclaiming that Asians had become too powerful and deserved to be evicted from the country. Like so many demagogues of the past, he was singling out a scapegoat in a quixotic quest for personal and political advantage. Most people discounted Matiba's comments, but his words still had the potential to cause tremendous harm.

Though black Africans clearly hold the most important positions in contemporary Kenya, racial feeling sometimes surfaces in strange ways. African Americans have flocked to Africa in recent years, hoping to find a connection to their own forebears and a link to their own past. Some of these observers have been disturbed by the pervasive poverty that often seems to override any racial connection that they might feel. A number have also spoken or written about their own discomfort with a lingering sense of inferiority on the part of some black Kenyans, which dates back to colonial times. Barack Obama, the child of a black African man and a white American woman, sought in the early 1990s to recapture a sense of his own past. He traveled to Kenya to meet members of his own family and to learn whatever he could about the father he barely knew. At one point in *Dreams from My Father*, his account of his quest, he writes of sitting with his half-sister Auma at the outdoor cafe at the New Stanley Hotel in Nairobi. This was, and remains, a watering hole for old-time colonials and their safari-bound counterparts today. Virtually all of the clientele is white. Obama and Auma were ignored, while a white American family just entering the cafe was taken care of quickly and courteously. Obama describes how Auma furiously flung a 100 shilling note to the ground and told the black waiter, "You should be ashamed of yourself. I don't care how many mouths you have to feed; you cannot treat your own people like dogs."

Keith Richburg, an African-American correspondent for the *Washington Post*, relates a similar story in *Out of America: A Black Man Confronts Africa*, his angry account of his experiences abroad. A fellow correspondent, also black, went to a popular restaurant at the Safari Park Hotel, just outside downtown Nairobi. This garish complex is a favorite of white visitors and ex-patriates who can afford to spend on one dinner a sum of money that would pay for food for an entire Kenyan family for a month. Waiting endlessly for orders to be taken, Richburg's friend finally complained to the manager, who said, "We didn't know who you were," apologetically assuming she and her black friends were Kenyan. "Here the colonial mentality runs deep," she concluded angrily. "But I don't want to wear an 'honorary white' sign over my head."

I suppose I was fortunate that I never encountered such racially charged discrimination aimed at black Africans when I was out with Kenyan friends. Perhaps my presence created a mixed group that was treated differently. Perhaps the parties I attended with African Americans in Nairobi were likewise mixed-race gatherings, where the ground rules necessarily changed. Even so, in my social interactions with African friends, I occasionally found myself more conscious of being white than I had ever been before.

I felt the same way in other parts of Africa. In South Africa, despite the remarkable efforts of Nelson Mandela and the government he formed, the separation between the races is still visible in large parts of the country. Suburbs of Johannesburg remain almost entirely white, while blacks flood into the downtown areas, and the township of Soweto remains entirely black. In Uganda and in Tanzania, I felt much as I did in Kenya whenever I wandered about on my own. Once again I was the outsider, the curiously colored stranger who somehow seemed vaguely out of place. As I ventured over to West Africa, I felt even further disconnected, for there I had the added disadvantage of knowing even less about the culture. In Côte d'Ivoire, my problems were compounded by language difficulties, where I had only my rudimentary French to help me find my way around.

In Ghana, however, I began to feel on firmer ground. As I traveled around the country, I came across large numbers of African Americans, far more than I ever encountered in Kenya, on a quest to find their own roots. In the castles at Cape Coast, we looked together at the dungeons where black slaves had been held before they were shipped abroad and speculated on the horrors of the trans-Atlantic passage that lay ahead. Then, in Accra, I went to visit the house where black American activist W.E.B. Du Bois spent the last years of his life. There, tagging along with an African-American tour group, I saw an inscription of the famous observation Du Bois made in 1903, in his eloquent account *Of the Dawn of Freedom*: "The problem of the twentieth century is the problem of the color line." He was pointing to the problems plaguing American society throughout its past, and still, I knew, plaguing the nation today. Yet those words had a special resonance in black Africa. For me in Ghana, Kenya, and the other parts of Africa I came to know, as for my African-American friends in the United States, the color line has not yet disappeared.

But there were moments when it seemed to fade. Several times during my stay in Kenya, I spoke at some length to Richard Leakey, the world-renowned paleontologist whose contributions created international interest in East Africa and sympathy for stopping the extermination of the elephant population. Later, Leakey became a central figure in the multiracial quest for political reform. Though Leakey, who is white, firmly denied any personal political ambitions, his reflections on his own role led to a telling comment about the larger issue of race. When I asked what it was like for him, born and raised in Kenya, to be white in a black country, he responded: "I think the answer to that would have to be if one thought of oneself as white, it would be tough. If one thinks of oneself as a Kenyan, it's no different for people who work here. And I don't think of myself as white at all. I'm just a person who's doing what I'm doing. I think that *is* an important distinction to make, and it may be hard to put across to people, but . . . I'm not conscious of color at all."

Leakey's words often echoed through my mind as I taught at the University of Nairobi or gave lectures to audiences in other parts of the country. In the classroom or in a larger arena, as I looked out at my African audience listening intently to what I was saying, I, too, was able to forget that my audience was black and I was not. Preoccupied by what I was trying to convey, and eager to learn how my listeners might respond, I could transcend earlier anxieties, and in those moments, the issue of race ceased in my mind to have any importance at all.

Yet race remains a troubling issue for most Americans. Books by authors such as Studs Terkel, assessing the patterns of recent years, question whether there has been real progress in our own society. Meanwhile, more and more white voters seem to be concerned about what they have come to call reverse discrimination and ponder the future of affirmative action. A national initiative on race during Bill Clinton's presidency sought to encourage the kind of dialogue that could perhaps help redeem the promise of the United States. But tensions remain fierce, and there is some evidence that the country is becoming more polarized than before. Even when we try to ignore the question of race, we've all come to realize that it simply won't go away.

My African sojourn forced me to reflect on my own attitudes about race. Those times when I felt self-conscious brought me back to my college friends and made me understand, at an emotional level, what I think Henry and Charlie must have experienced as outsiders in the world of the mid-1960s. They never complained, and only rarely reflected, with me at least, on the occasional awkwardness they felt. But that experience of being different helped define the choices they made, just as being white in a black country helped me understand better the complicated issues that face Africans, and Americans, in our effort to deal with the problems that affect us all.

Marital Ties

When I first met my neighbor Mary, I wondered about the man sitting in a corner of her living room who said nothing at all. He seemed preoccupied with his newspaper and, while he occasionally acknowledged my entrance by wrinkling his brow, he invariably returned to his reading as soon as he could. I didn't need to have any contact with him, for there were plenty of other people in the apartment. Mary was usually there, along with her daughters, Sheila and Joy. After work, Kimathi, Mary's stepson, returned to the flat. There were also a couple of young women from Mary's rural home living in the apartment, doing the cooking and housework in return for room and board and a chance to go to school. And there were the inevitable visitors, the family members and friends who also stayed in the tiny two-bedroom flat like the one Sara and I lived in next door.

After a couple of weeks, I asked Mary about the silent figure who had staked out his claim to the one easy chair in the room. "Who is he?" I asked. "What is he doing in your flat?"

"He's my husband," Mary said, and left it at that.

I found myself puzzled by her reticence and her response. But I was just beginning to get to know her as a friend, and I was not yet ready to pry further. Still, I now found myself wondering about the marriage patterns and conjugal customs in this East African land. It seemed a strange way to treat a husband, almost pretending he didn't exist. I knew there's always much outsiders don't see in a marriage; I had been through a divorce myself some years before, and remembered all too well the silent hostility that could pervade a home and poison the patterns of everyday life. But this relationship— if it could be called that—seemed different from what I remembered of my own life. In this case, the strange man seemed like an extraneous object.

There was no visible hostility, not even in the small sliver of space he inhabited. It was as if he wasn't really there.

Several weeks later, I learned a little more. Mary and I had gone to a university function in my car and, as we drove home, we began to talk. I asked a couple of leading questions, and Mary, usually gregarious, evidently felt comfortable enough to respond. Sitting outside in the dark parking lot, she told me about the complications in her life. She and her husband were estranged, she said, and had been for some time. But divorce was out of the question in Kenyan society. Legally possible, it was simply not practical and, even if she could see a case through to a successful end, it would leave her an outsider in her own culture. Women operated at a serious disadvantage, and she stood to lose everything she had, even her children. And so the two of them inhabited the same space, slept in the same bed, and had absolutely nothing to do with one another. "How can you live like that?" I wanted to know. Like most married couples, Sara and I had our difficulties from time to time, and I have an often unhealthy capacity to hold on to a grudge, but this made me look like the friendliest person in the world.

We talked for about an hour that evening, and the conversation continued for the entire year. As the months passed, I learned more and more about Mary's life, and through it about the patterns that governed the lives of Kenyan women and men. Mary's case was not all that strange, I discovered, as I queried other friends, or simply watched them in their offices and homes.

Midway through our stay in Kenya, Sara had the American students she was leading on the semester abroad do a project that revealed a good deal to me about family patterns in a rural town. While I was working in Nairobi, she and her students were staying in rural Kaimosi, a heavily populated, poverty-stricken community in Western Province, not far from Lake Victoria. In an effort to get a first-hand glimpse at the way people in the countryside lived, each student resided for three and a half weeks with a Kenyan family, usually in a house that lacked both electricity and running water. As they settled in, Sara bought twenty disposable cameras, and gave one to each student to give to the wife of the family, with a request that she take pictures of the people and things most important to her. Though none of these women had ever held a camera in her hands, they all quickly learned how to point and shoot. After the photographs were developed, each student was to show them to the woman who had taken the pictures and ask her to provide a caption indicating what was going on.

The pictures provided a fascinating glimpse of rural life. There were dozens of images of children and plenty of shots of corn fields and cows. Many of the women photographed dishes drying in the kitchen, for cleanliness was an important value in their lives. Others photographed their outdoor toilet—known in Kiswahili as the *choo*. Most revealing, out of several hundred pictures in all, there were only two or three shots of their husbands.

I slowly realized that, in many families, both in Nairobi and in rural towns, the husbands were often away. Some went to look for work elsewhere, though jobs were hard to find. Others spent the day drinking in the bar. Even when they were around, there was little concept of companionate marriage as we have come to embrace it back home. Men were necessary, the women seemed to acknowledge, and virtually every Kenyan woman expected to marry and have children. But beyond that, the men didn't seem that important to them, even if they retained power and control over women's lives.

In Kenya today, men hold most of the really important positions in politics and public life and dominate the world of business and commercial affairs. And they do as they choose, with the full sanction of the culture, in their private and personal lives. Women remain second-class citizens. I asked Mary to tell me about Kenyan families and queried my University of Nairobi students—men and women both—about their hopes and expectations for spouses, jobs, and careers. I asked colleagues about everything from circumcision patterns to the customs governing divorce. What emerged was an impressionistic sense of the patterns of daily life.

The Kenyan constitution clearly forbids discrimination on the basis of sex, but that injunction has about as much force as the biblical ban on stealing in a country where corruption is rampant. Women remain subservient to men in virtually everything they do. Up-country, where traditional patterns predating colonial days still govern their lives, women are expected to bear as many babies as they can, fetch water for their families, and tend the fields while their husbands go their own way. Many of the men spend endless hours drinking bottle after bottle of Tusker beer at the neighborhood bar, often a small shack with a corrugated metal roof. When other men leave the villages to seek work elsewhere, either in Nairobi or in neighboring towns, some may start new families without bothering to inform wives back home. Yet even when they are away, they remain in control of the patterns of family life. Their wives enjoy a measure of welcome autonomy as long as the men are gone, but snap back into their accustomed roles as soon as their husbands return.

I saw that pattern unfold almost daily. On one occasion, I invited Rose, my Kiswahili teacher, to our home for dinner. Over a period of months, she and I had spent at least an hour a day in class, most of that time in conversation about everything from the weather to the intricacies of Kenyan culture. These conversations were in Kiswahili, of course, and I'm sure I missed much of what Rose said. But she was animated and lively as she talked to me about her home, her family, her children, and her life. I felt as though we had a bond between us, and I looked forward to our daily sessions. At first, as we spoke about dinner, we planned to include a male language teacher who had taught me for a short while, but his wife became ill, and he was unable to attend. At that point, Rose asked if her husband, who also worked in Nairobi, could come along. I said of course.

As we drove in my car to the office where he worked, Rose was as lively as ever, chatting amiably about whatever came to mind. As soon as we picked her husband up, she fell silent, and her silence persisted for the entire evening. Sara and I tried repeatedly to turn the conversation to topics I knew she liked to talk about, but we ended up with a triangular discussion that left Rose out altogether. In company, with her husband present, she deferred to him, even when we were reflecting on the difficulties of language teaching, an area in which he had no expertise but still held strong opinions, which he shared vocally, to our dismay. Rose was as frozen as a deer caught in the headlights of a car.

At the end of what soon became a tiresome evening, I drove Rose and her husband home. He asked to be let off before we reached their apartment, so that he could visit the family of a friend who had died. As soon as he got out of the car, Rose became animated again and, for the remainder of the drive home, was the same exuberant woman I had known before.

Some months later, Sara and I visited Lonah, a craftswoman who regularly taught Sara's students how to make banana-fiber baskets in Kaimosi. When Sara had visited Lonah before, her husband had usually been gone, working at a reasonably well-paying job for the Kenya national railroad network in Nairobi. He had often stayed in the big city for months at a time, coming back only occasionally. Lonah had seemed comfortable with the arrangement. He sent some money home, and she tended her small fields of crops and took care of her children as she chose.

This time, though, there was trouble. Lonah had written Sara a letter saying that her husband had retired and had returned home for good. He had appropriated a small amount of money Sara had given her to build a tiny *duka*— a shop selling such items as soap, eggs, matches, and candy to the neighbors. Lonah assumed he had spent the money on liquor, and recognized that it was forever gone. Even worse, he had beaten her on a number of occasions. At the time she wrote, she had fled to her mother's home, while she decided what to do.

Well aware that such separations were hard to sustain, when we arrived we checked first at her own house, a modest but attractive brick structure not far from the main road to Kisumu. As I had anticipated, she was there, having decided, she said, to make things work with her husband again. Like Rose, she chatted comfortably until he came inside and joined the group. Then she clammed up, eager only to get Sara aside to secretly pass on her private bank account number for any future gifts that could be kept safe from her husband's greedy hands.

Marriage in Kenya, I came to realize, still unfolds according to time-treasured rituals. Patterns vary according to ethnic group, but the basic configurations are country-wide. Virtually everywhere, a suitor pays a dowry to the family of his prospective bride. The woman is expected to leave her father's home and go live with her husband's family after marrying, and compensation is required for the economic loss. And so the inevitable haggling begins, resulting in a final bridal price of fifteen or twenty or fifty cows and goats, or some combination of livestock and cash. I had expected this dickering over dowry among the nomadic people up north, like the Turkana, who spend their lives following their wandering cows, or from the Maasai, who believe that they have a God-given right to every cow that inhabits the earth. I was surprised to see the same negotiations taking place among Kikuyu and Meru friends who were much more urbanized than the Turkana or Maasai, and in other groups around the country. Even a professional woman like Mary had a dowry that had to be paid when she got married. She had not been wholly comfortable about the prospect of being sold off for a couple of scraggly cows, she told me, but this was a custom she could live with, and so the price had been paid.

While Mary was willing to accommodate her family over the payment of a dowry, she felt she could not do that with circumcision. These days, critics in the West, and some activists in developing countries, have brought the issue of female circumcision to growing attention. It is a fraught subject, pitting local custom against human rights. There have been debates about many aspects of the issue—about whether outsiders have the standing to criticize; about the limits of cultural relativism; about whether women fleeing the practice are eligible for political asylum in the West; and about whether female circumcision, which can include the radical clitoridectomy, is, as critics say, genital mutilation, inflicting life-long pain, suffering, and serious health risks.

Most, but not all, Kenyan men, I learned, are circumcised. The Luos near Lake Victoria do not practice the custom, and some Kenyans say this disqualifies prominent Luo politicians like Raila Odinga from ever becoming president. They consider the failure to experience this rite of passage an abomination. How could the country survive, they ask, being governed by an uncircumcised man who is still a boy? Families of uncircumcised boys, or boys not circumcised in the traditional way, find themselves at a distinct disadvantage in their communities. Moses, a close friend of ours in Kaimosi, served as a prominent diplomat in the Kenyan Foreign Service, with postings in Paris, Toronto, and a variety of other places. On the walls of his home are numerous pictures of him and his wife with the Pope and with dignitaries from around the world. At the conclusion of his diplomatic career, which came with mandatory retirement at the age of fifty-five for public officials, he returned to his village home, hoping to run for Parliament or some other political office. But his boys had been circumcised in a hospital and not in the forest, and some members of the community considered him unfit for further consideration, other qualifications notwithstanding.

Circumcision of young boys takes place at periodic intervals in villages around the country. Every several years, adolescents, ranging from nine to fourteen, retreat to the forest to learn the customs of their own people, culminating with the surgical cut, done by an elder who has been practicing his craft for years. Among the Tiriki, the people we got to know well in Western Province, boys are not permitted to cry out or acknowledge any pain at all, at the risk of embarrassment that will ruin the experience then and remain with them the rest of their lives. After healing occurs, the boys return to the village wearing woven, feather-covered masks they have made and dance together in a public acknowledgment of having come of age.

I understood male circumcision as a rite of passage. Like most Americans, I viewed female circumcision in an altogether different light. I had read and heard authors such as Alice Walker rail against what they called a barbaric custom. I had grimaced as Kenyan friends related stories of radical surgical procedures, performed without anesthesia, that were designed to limit sexual pleasure for women and often caused complications in childbirth, but which were considered crucial for girls coming of age. Still, I had not yet confronted the full range of opinion on the question.

I didn't have to wait long. Soon after I arrived at the University of Nairobi, I attended a history-department seminar in which an American graduate student who had been doing research in Meru presented her findings on circumcision to a mixed audience of women and men. She herself was clearly uncomfortable with the custom, and was now trying to explain its extraordinary persistence. Under pressure from various church groups, the Kenyan government over the years has tried unsuccessfully to stop the practice, though in neighboring Tanzania, which is culturally close to Kenya, female circumcision is becoming much less common. As I heard some of my colleagues speak, I began to understand the place this custom plays in Kenyan society. Many of the educated women remained silent. But many of their male counterparts spoke out forcefully, endorsing a tradition that they said was a necessary rite of passage for the continuity of cultural values they viewed as vital for them all. A woman was not a woman, they argued, unless she submitted to the patterns prescribed in the past by the elders of her village home. Some women living in villages up-country still agree. Circumcision, they suggest, helps buttress gender relationships that are beginning to change, and provides an important link with traditions of the past.

Mary, however, would have none of it. Somewhere along the line, as a young girl in Meru, she had decided that she was not going to be circumcised. With the same determination that helped her overcome obstacles in her academic career, she had refused to submit to what the elders wanted. The prevailing assumption was that once a girl was circumcised, she could get married; Mary believed that some women would use that as an excuse to get her to drop out of school, which she was determined not to do. She knew, she told me, that "circumcision . . . is a cultural rite. It's supposed to be upheld. It's something that makes a woman a woman, respectable." Her father and other family members insisted on it being done. "If she's not circumcised, then she's going to get out of hand," they said. "You can't control her." But none of that made any difference to her, as she recalled "a night where I fought up to the morning, and I was ready to cut everybody to pieces." At the end of the battle, she reported the episode to the village chief, who understood the cultural changes that were taking place and took her side. She remained uncut, but a legacy of hostility lingered. And to this day, Mary stays away from her village at circumcision time, out of fear that still-irritated neighbors might capture her and perform the procedure against her will.

"How did you come to get married?" I asked. She had met her husband while she was teaching, she told me, after taking her advanced examinations at the end of secondary school. He was a teacher too, at that time, and they saw a good deal of one another. "He was a fantastic man then, I guess," she said with a rueful smile. "He was good. I don't know what happened to him." When she went on to the University of Nairobi, she had no other serious boy friends. The two of them spent most of their time together and after, five years, they finally got married.

"What went wrong?" I wanted to know. Things were fine at first, she said. Sheila was born after they had been married for a while and, several years later, Joy was born. Around this time, though, Mary began to notice a difference in her husband. He spent more and more time away from home, and seemed preoccupied when he was around. Only later did she realize that he was constructing another life that left her out altogether. He told her that his work in the Office of the President required his posting out of town, far to the north, where telephone service would be intermittent at best. He would be away for months at a time, he told her, and would simply be out of touch for the duration. Mary sensed that something was wrong, but acquiesced. Women are often left alone in Kenya, and the pattern that her husband proposed was not significantly different from the model followed in many families she knew. It wasn't what she wanted, to be sure, but perhaps, she thought, it would work out in the end.

But things failed to improve. Her husband came home less and less frequently and, when he was around, their relationship deteriorated even further.

Like many Kenyan couples, they seemed to be living separate lives, and in this case there was virtually no interaction.

Finally, Mary learned what was going on. Her father-in-law, back in her home village, was dying, and when he came to Nairobi for medical treatment, Mary was the one who took care of him. They became closer, even though Mary thought his family had long held a grudge against her for not being circumcised, and he began to confide in her. Her husband had come to the family several years before, he said, and told his parents he wanted to take a second wife. He had become involved with a woman at work and wanted to marry her.

Polygamy is still sometimes practiced in Kenya. Mary's own father had fathered four children with his first wife, even while entering into quiet liaisons with other women in the village. Then he got entangled with a young woman who worked in his own house and, when she became pregnant, he decided to marry her. Local custom permits this, although the Christian church does not. Taking a second wife is not common, except among the Maasai and in Islamic areas on the coast, but it does occur.

"Why did your father want a second wife?" I wondered. Mary thought the reason was that he had only had four children with her mother and, by Kenyan standards, that was far too few. In a country where children provide a kind of social security in old age, the more family members around the better, at least for an older man looking toward the end of his life.

In some polygamous arrangements, the second—and usually younger—wife gets most of the attention. The husband may move in with her, or spend most of his time with her, at the expense of the woman who had been with him at the start. Some years before, I had read Senegalese author Mariama Bâ's eloquent novel *So Long a Letter*, in which the older wife records the pain felt when her husband abruptly decides to take a second wife, the best friend of their young daughter. This was a work from West, and not East, Africa. But the human emotions of sorrow and suffering were similar to what I saw among Kenyan friends.

Some polygamous marriages I observed seemed to work relatively comfortably. Njoroge, the oldest son of my friend Justus, had two wives and when he built a large stone house in his father's compound, he constructed a main hallway near the front door, with identical wings—one for each wife—on either side. Each wing was like a separate apartment, with a living room, bedroom, and kitchen. Each wife cooked her own food and took care of her own children, and I frequently saw the two together on my visits to the family.

"Where do you sleep?" I asked Njoroge once.

"I look to see what each wife is cooking, and then I make up my mind," he said with a smile.

In rural villages, the pattern may be somewhat different, and the wives may have separate huts. In some cases, the husband may live in a house of his own, with the autonomy to decide each night where to sleep. In the case of Mary's father, he continued to live with his first wife, in the house they had shared together for many years. His new wife had a separate house in the compound that quickly filled up, for as Mary noted of her father, "He goes to visit and make babies and comes back." By the time he was done, there were eight more children to feed.

There were inevitable frictions in the arrangement. "My reaction to my father's getting a second wife was hostile," Mary recalled. When her father went off traveling, she and her brother fought with the new wife, who was about her own age, and Mary's mother took her daughter's side. Later, as the children from the second union began to appear, there was further conflict, for the necessary school fees cut into the family's ability to pay for Mary's education.

Mary, like most Kenyan woman, was no fan of polygamy, even if her own father had followed the practice. And, she told me, there was one crucial difference between what her father and her husband had done. Mary had been married in church, in a Christian wedding, and despite the absorption by most denominations of traditional, pre-colonial customs, churches in Kenya forbade a man from having more than one wife. In much the same way that American clerics lashed out at the polygamous Mormons, even as they moved further and further west, Kenyan Christians have long tried to end the custom of multiple wives. Men married in the village, according to local custom, can avoid the church injunction, and some men have taken more than one wife. But for those, like Mary, married in church, there was now an ethical—and legal—sanction that could be invoked.

Mary became closer and closer to her father-in-law in the months before he died. Her husband, preoccupied with his own affairs, stayed away. As Mary struggled to cope with her children, her studies, and her ailing patient, she began to get a fuller picture of her husband's secret life. A formal second marriage may never have occurred, but an informal union was firmly in place, even if forbidden by the church. Now the behavior of his prodigal son began to bother Mary's father-in-law as well and, just before he died, he cast a curse on his son.

A curse is a pretty powerful weapon, I learned. Mary's husband, like her a practicing Presbyterian, found himself laboring under a spell recognized by his own community, whether members were Christians or not. When he learned about the curse, he apparently had second thoughts about what he had done, and wanted to make amends. He began coming around Mary's apartment more frequently, indicating he wanted to live there full-time.

By this point, Mary wanted nothing more to do with him. She knew about the other woman and had heard that the union had produced a child as well. She was ready to avoid her husband altogether for the rest of her life. Resourceful as ever, she had acquired the apartment she lived in on her own when she began to teach at the University of Nairobi and now, she decided, she needed nothing from her husband at all. Even if he returned to the flat, it would be as if he was out of her life altogether. Despite the rebuff, her husband pointed out that they *were* still married and he insisted on coming back.

And so they lived in a kind of chilly neutrality, without even a shred of communication between them. Mary's husband occasionally took the girls out, or talked with them about what they were doing, but there was little interaction with anyone. He took most of his meals elsewhere, and paid nothing for food for his family, telling his daughter Sheila that since he didn't eat there, he saw no reason to pay. In a kind of guerrilla warfare, Mary and the girls took light bulbs out of the sockets when they went to bed, so that he wouldn't wake them up when he came home later and tried to turn on all the lamps.

I found myself returning again and again to the question I had asked Mary when I first learned about her husband: "How can you live like that?"

As Mary came over to our apartment more frequently, sometimes in the morning, sometimes late at night, she tried to answer that question. Over a period of months, I learned more and more about the messy situation from which there seemed no escape. Sara and I both knew about the difficulties of divorce in the United States but now learned how much more painful it was in Kenya. A divorced woman, Mary told me, was a social outcast. People would accuse her of not being accommodating enough to her husband's legitimate demands, and would keep her at arm's length if she left her marriage. It was one thing for a man to leave his wife, whether permanently or for a period of time. Indeed, in Muslim culture, a divorce could be negotiated by the man simply telling his wife "I divorce you" four times in succession. It was a little more difficult, though still acceptable, for a man to extricate himself in non-Muslim parts of the country. But in a male-dominated community, it was almost impossible for a woman to go off on her own.

Custodial arrangements reflected the larger cultural patterns. Because a man had paid a dowry for his wife, he was entitled to everything the marriage produced, and that included the children. A woman rejected by her husband was expected to slink back alone to her village, a failure in the world's eyes. Only in Muslim communities on the coast did a divorced woman retain custody of her children. On one occasion, Simon, a Maasai friend, was sitting with Sara's students as they were listening to a lecture on the patterns of coastal life. When he learned that children in a Muslim home severed by divorce departed with the mother, he was appalled. If a man had paid a dowry and parted with precious cows, he argued vigorously, like a lawyer in a court-room, he had a right to the kids.

Mary had no intention of going back to Meru, regardless of how many cows may have changed hands. But it hardly seemed worth the trouble to her to expend considerable effort and expense to obtain a divorce that might not be beneficial to her in the end.

I did my best to keep my mouth shut. I still wondered how she could tol-erate what was fundamentally an intolerable state of affairs. How could she share a bed, I asked myself, with someone for whom she had such contempt? I sometimes joked about the phantom in the living room, the flesh and blood fixture who seldom moved. And, as the year progressed, we talked about the future configurations of her life.

Mary wanted to get a Ph.D. No one in her village had ever received one, and it was her own special goal. The University of Nairobi awarded doctoral degrees, but the process was interminable and, in the departments I knew best, virtually no one managed to complete all requirements successfully. Many faculty members seemed to make students jump through hoops that would have tripped a prize-winning scholar. There was little sense of encour-aging a student to finish as quickly as possible. Eager to cobble together a liv-ing as best they could, some of my colleagues were so busy with other jobs outside the university that they had little time for their students. They some-times neglected papers and theses submitted for months at a time before re-turning them at long last with nit-picking demands for change. The only way for aspiring academics to move forward was to go abroad. Some of Mary's colleagues studied in Great Britain. More headed for the United States.

Mary began to apply to American graduate schools during the year I lived in Kenya. As she contemplated the prospect of leaving the country, she began to worry about how to accommodate her children. Many Kenyan men simply left for four or five years, returning home after they had completed their doc-toral degrees. Women, with substantial responsibilities at home, left less of-ten and, if they did depart, had the added complication of figuring out how to maintain family life. Mary could have sent her girls back to the village, where a large extended family would have taken care of them for months or even years. Another possibility she considered was to leave by herself and send for her daughters once she had settled in.

From my western perspective, those options bothered me. The girls were too bright and too eager to learn to leave them in what seemed to me to be an unsatisfactory limbo. Feeling that I now knew Mary well enough to voice my honest opinion, I tentatively suggested that, if she won a fellowship and man-aged to study abroad, she should take Joy and Sheila with her at the same time.

At that point, Mary began to worry about what her husband might do. If she announced that she was leaving for the United States over his objections, she might lose custody of the girls forever. Her husband could seize them at any time, and she might never see them again.

With a sense of relief, I watched Mary reason with herself about issues that were difficult to confront. I was encouraging, but I also sometimes wondered whether I was being too manipulative. Was I applying my own sense of family values to a situation where they didn't really apply? Did I have any business telling Mary what to do? I never fully answered those questions to myself, just tried to do what felt best to me.

Mary decided she should take the girls if she could. To that end, she realized that her only real hope was to get the divorce—and custody of her children—that she had deemed impossible just a few months before.

To achieve that, Mary began to do the necessary detective work. Astute inquiries gave her a better sense of her husband's extramarital life. He had, she learned, become involved with a secretary with whom he worked. He evidently told this woman that he had been married before, but was now divorced, and his wife had gone to America and was out of the picture. He had fathered two children by that informal union, and Mary managed to find birth certificates acknowledging his paternity. Now she had what she needed to go to court.

Divorce cases are seldom easy. My own took longer than I care to remember, and left me exhausted and drained. Even with no-fault divorce statutes and an effort to expedite the process, reaching a final settlement is often difficult. But the problems we have in the United States pale against efforts to make the Kenyan court system respond. Women face the heaviest burden of proof in this paternalistic country, where the very act of objecting to a union is viewed as a hostile deed. Though Mary had an airtight case, in which she could document both adultery and neglect, she still had to move it through the channels of the court.

Mary was one of those people who always had time for everyone, and now it was time for others to help her. She found a lawyer friend who agreed to take the case. With proper legal assistance, they managed to get the case on the docket of the most sympathetic judge. Then it was necessary to endure the endless delays that can frustrate the most patient petitioner at the court. Mary initiated legal proceedings in the spring, several months before Sara and I were slated to go home. Naively optimistic, I hoped the case could be concluded before we departed, but it soon became clear that such a solution was out of the question. I remained anxious, but Mary wasn't worried because graduate study in the United States was still more than a year away.

As August approached, and our year in Kenya came to an end, Mary remained calm. With the same patience that had allowed her to keep herself together and respond to all the demands on her as her marriage was falling apart, she focused on her ultimate goal of graduate education, convinced that everything would work out in the end.

It did. A year later, at just about the time she got word of her acceptance with a fellowship to a doctoral program at Michigan State University, her divorce became final. After endless legal delays, she was free at last, with sole custody of her children. Her husband was required to pay the fairly substantial sum of 2,000 Kenyan shillings—about $30—each month, but Mary knew she would never see the money and didn't intend to make a fuss. At long last, she had the freedom to leave, and to take the girls with her. Once worried about the stigma of divorce, she now steeled herself not to care about what her friends and colleagues thought. As she declared, reflecting on the external reaction she had feared: "I told myself loudly that this society that I'm so worried about does not live in my house." More than ever before, she was eager to start a new life.

Mary gave me some sense of what it was like being a professional woman in Nairobi. Over the course of my stay in Kenya, I spent a good deal of time watching women in the rural villages hauling water, tending crops, cooking, and caring for their children, while their husbands were either absent or otherwise engaged. I began to read the literature about the burdens women assumed in much of Africa and in most developing countries. And I came to realize that simple existence was sometimes just as difficult for women caught up in cities. The support structures of rural towns were missing in the city slums, where crime became more of a problem and alcohol was even easier to obtain.

Life was hard for poor, working-class women unable to find jobs. But it was equally difficult for more educated women who faced all the burdens of maintaining households in addition to holding down their jobs. When I asked Mary to reflect on the patterns of her own life, she answered, "Being a professional woman is just more hardship, I would say. It's not easy going." She was expected to do everything for everybody, and this took enormous amounts of time, even though she had household help. "You are almost everything," she said. "You find yourself at the end of the day, you are almost collapsing, over the load that you've been carrying the whole day." Often her duties—teaching extra classes to support her children—kept her away until late at night. I grew used to seeing the fatigue in her face.

And, I gradually came to understand, Mary is not alone. Women still face a real uphill battle in their quest for equality in Kenya and in many other parts of Africa.

Sexism remains firmly entrenched in Kenya. In 1979, Parliament rejected a measure that would have allowed a woman to object legally if her husband took a second wife. It had also stated that "No spouse shall have any right to inflict corporal punishment on the other." Parliament shelved the bill, calling it "un-African." One member of the legislative chamber said that relations between a husband and wife were private, and should remain unregulated by the court. Another parliamentarian declared that passage of such a law "would be throwing our customs to the dogs." Years later, the bill remained unpassed.

In 1985, the position of Kenyan women was highlighted as the United Nations sponsored an international conference in Nairobi to assess progress made in what it called the women's decade. "Coming to Africa to make such an assessment, it struck me at the time," American newspaper correspondent Blaine Harden commented later, "made as much sense as going to Beirut to study world peace." The conference ran its course, just like its successor in the following decade, and little changed. Approximately 70 percent of Kenya's female population remained rural in the 1990s, with many of the women illiterate. In urban areas, women held only 20 percent of all jobs, and were regularly paid less than their male counterparts. But there was a growing sense of disaffection providing some pressure for change. Women began to band together in a variety of self-help organizations to try to improve the conditions they faced.

One articulate reform voice belonged to Wangari Maathai. A biologist who served two terms as head of the National Council of Women of Kenya, she had first spoken out in opposition to the country's strict marriage laws in 1981. For those efforts, she was jailed for contempt. Later, she developed the Green Belt movement to try to empower ordinary people, women included, to effect changes in their own environment by planting trees. This was a subversive effort, she understood. "African governments do not encourage and have not yet accepted the fact that people can direct their own destiny," she said. "They want to guide them and they want to be followed blindly. They do not want their people informed or organized because organized groups threaten their position."

Maathai ran up against the establishment in 1989, when she challenged the government's plan to build a sixty-story commercial building in Uhuru Park, a green space running through the center of the city. Political leaders wanted to house the headquarters of the Kenya African National Union (KANU), the only legal party at the time, in the new structure, which would also have featured a thirty-foot statue of President Moi. Requesting an environmental impact statement, Maathai filed suit to stop construction. The courts rejected the motion on a technicality and told her to seek assistance from the Attorney General. Not unexpectedly, he refused to help. Female activists in Kenya often found themselves with few friends, and Maathai now faced stinging criticism from both the president and *Maendeleo ya Wanawake*, a national organization whose Kiswahili name translates as Progress for Women. Worried that Maathai's example could complicate its own efforts, *Maendeleo ya Wanawake* responded to governmental pressure by demanding that she be expelled from the ruling party. Soon after, the Green Belt movement was evicted from its offices in a government-owned building.

Yet Maathai won in the end, and in so doing demonstrated that an articulate female activist could indeed make a difference. Foreign donors responded to her campaign and announced that the $200 million price tag for the building was more than Kenya could afford. Faced with a loss of funding, the government shelved the project and Uhuru Park remained intact. Even so, a legacy of bitterness remained.

As I lived and worked in Kenya, I was conscious all the time of the burdens most women faced. As funding for education dried up, and students were told that they were going to have to pay at least part of their expenses to attend the university, educators and other commentators voiced fears that this would change the gender balance of those in attendance. Faced with the need to provide school fees, their argument ran, many families would be willing to pay for the education of a man, but not for the advanced schooling of a woman. As I left Kenya in the summer of 1996, that pattern was beginning to occur.

The female students I taught were every bit as good as their male counterparts. Like the men, some of the women were outgoing, and others were shy. Some came to class prepared, while others made it clear that they had better things to do. On balance, the women proved to be just as vocal in class discussions as the men. Despite that veneer of equality, cultural patterns persisted. Although most of the male students accepted their female colleagues as their peers, they still clung to more traditional expectations when they thought about getting married and settling down. They wanted wives who would treat them with the same deference and respect they remembered in their families back home. And the persistence of those patterns makes it difficult to anticipate either rapid or fundamental transformations soon.

During the year I taught in Kenya, I began to wonder if real change would ever occur. I was at first amused, then disturbed at the reaction to the Kenyan delegation to the international women's conference held in China, in Beijing. The local press had a field day as it described what was going on. First, it ridiculed the female cabinet minister who headed the delegation for bringing a hairdresser with her to the conference. Her argument that it was important to be presentable at a top-level meeting of this kind fell on deaf ears. Even more important was the hostility to the debates going on in Beijing about such practices as female circumcision. The reaction was much like the response to the bill seeking to amend the marriage law a decade and a half before. There was nothing of value for Africa in these discussions, many of the reporters (virtually all of them male) seemed to say. African men know best, and African women should know their place.

Yet times are changing. When I returned to Kenya a year later, I found a woman, Charity Ngilu, running for the presidency. No one thought she had much of a chance. No one thought any opponent of Daniel arap Moi had much of a chance. But she made a fight of it, though she lost in the end, and her presence demonstrated a political climate that was different from what it had been before.

Even more important, for me, was Mary's example. She had undergone a major transformation in the year we lived next door. From a passive acceptance of conditions she thought she couldn't challenge, she had decided to fight back and, in the process, regained control of her own life. Mary provided a model for me of the possibilities of change.

Sickness Unto Death

One morning, Mary, our neighbor and friend, knocked on our door and told us that her thirteen-year-old niece up-country, whom we had met when she visited Nairobi, had suddenly gotten a headache and died. She had suffered from problems of dizziness brought on by double vision, and had sought medical care in Nairobi, but simple X rays had detected nothing serious, and her dizziness had disappeared. Then one weekend, after she had returned home, she came back from Sunday school alone, ate something, and lay down. Her parents found her weak and frothing at the mouth. By the time they got her to a hospital, she was dead. She may have had a cerebral hemorrhage, but she lived far from the city, and no autopsy was ever done.

Illness is visible everywhere in Kenya today. Sara and I encountered sick people all the time, and not all of them recovered. Death at a premature age is far more common in Africa than in our world at home. Most Kenyan families we knew lost at least one member while we were there. Serious illness was simply part of Kenyan life.

The basic demographic patterns relating to disease and death in this part of the world are horrifying. Even as the Kenyan population soars—doubling every twenty years—the mortality rate remains inordinately high. AIDS has become the scourge of Africa, and Kenya has been hit hard by the plague. But tens of thousands of other people also battle with malaria, and more of them succumb to the disease than die of AIDS. Other ailments, such as cholera and typhoid, all but eradicated in the United States, still cause numerous fatalities as well. Africa remains the part of the world where children are most likely to die before the age of five and adults are least likely to survive beyond the age of fifty, and Kenya is part of this grim picture. Starvation may be less common than in Somalia or Ethiopia, but malnutrition weakens many of those with meager resources and leaves them all the more vulnerable to the fatal diseases that inevitably strike them down.

We were lucky. We remained relatively healthy in Kenya as we watched friends and acquaintances suffer from serious and frequently debilitating illnesses. But, as we helped Sara's American students navigate their way through the Kenyan health system, in the face of real and imagined ailments, we caught a glimpse of the problems of trying to maintain health standards and accommodate patients in a developing land. In the United States today, we grumble about the bureaucratic inconveniences imposed by the health maintenance organizations that complicate our lives. In many other parts of the world, people cannot even comprehend the sanitized but effective care we take for granted.

In Kenya, Sara and I worried most about malaria. This is the world's most prevalent parasitic disease, and it seems to be getting worse all the time. Several decades ago, killing mosquitoes through an international spraying program promised to wipe out the epidemic, but the insects soon built up resistance to the chemical sprays at the same time that the disease itself became resistant to drugs, such as chloroquine, that people took as both a preventative and a cure. There are currently an estimated 300 to 500 million cases annually, with deaths estimated at between 1.5 and 2.7 million each year. In Africa alone, the World Health Organization estimates that 88 million people have malaria. Some ten thousand travelers return home from malarial regions each year and become ill with the disease.

Before traveling to Africa, I was afraid of getting a malady that would cause progressively worse bouts of fever and chills and recur for the rest of my life. Images from old films of feverish patients growing weaker and weaker ran through my mind. And the treatment was hardly likely to be better. I imagined myself growing yellow from the quinine or atabrine or whatever one was supposed to take when the disease finally hit. Despite a deep-rooted aversion to medicine I might not need, prophylaxis seemed like a good idea. When I had served in the Peace Corps in the Philippines, I had dutifully swallowed a large red pill once a week, and those evidently did the trick. I was ready to take the same tablets, but now there were apparently better drugs to be had.

The first several times I went to Kenya, I took something called mefloquine, sold under the trade name of Lariam. It, too, seemed to work, for I managed to avoid malaria. When I attended a Fulbright orientation conference in Washington, D.C., before departing to teach for the year in Nairobi, a physician talked at length about various methods of prophylaxis. But we were told by other officials that it was Fulbright policy that we *must* take Lariam or we would not be given our grants. I signed a piece of paper to that effect, and began to take the drug.

Once in Kenya, however, I began to hear doubts about the drug I was about to take for a whole year. Non-Americans charged that the Centers for Disease Control in the United States endorsed this strong but dangerous prophylactic because it was American-made and, also, because it was least likely to result in lawsuits from travelers who returned home with the disease. Americans taking the drug sometimes talked about the side effects of Lariam: dizziness, strange dreams, and depression were among the symptoms that could occur.

Before long, I began to experience all of them. Or so I thought. It was a stressful time, to be sure. Finding a place to live had taken its toll. Sara was preoccupied with her students. Meanwhile, the University of Nairobi was already experiencing the problems that would soon lead to its closure for several months. When I began to feel anxious and unsettled, I ignored all other causes and became convinced that I was suffering from the symptoms of the drug.

"Stop taking Lariam," Sara said sensibly. At one level, that seemed like a terrifying step—challenging medical authority and risking my health as well. But the more I thought about it, the better the advice seemed. I forgot about the Fulbright injunction and began to take daily doses of proguanil, sold without prescription overseas as Paludrine, along with a dose of chloroquine once a week, a common combination at the time in Kenya. And I began to feel better.

At the same time, I realized that lots of people in Kenya got malaria and recovered quickly. Our neighbors and friends all had had bouts with the disease, had taken the medication prescribed, and had recuperated fully.

Malaria *could* be deadly, of course. A few years ago, a student on another institution's foreign-study program had been staying in Lamu, a small island in the Indian Ocean up the coast from Mombasa. She had gotten a particularly virulent strain of malaria that lodged in her brain, and she had died before she could get the kind of medical help available in a larger city. Sara was terrified that such a disaster could strike her program at any time, and so, even as we joked about students who thought that they had malaria every time they had a fever, we knew it was a deadly possibility.

My first encounter with the Kenyan health-care system came when two of Sara's students became sick. Elly began to feel dizzy while in Lamu. She could have been having the same kind of reaction to Lariam I had. Or she might have been suffering from the stress of adjustment to a new environment. Nonetheless, a local Lamu physician prescribed malaria medication in the characteristic first step taken to treat any ailment. The medicine didn't work, probably because Elly didn't really have malaria, and she continued to feel sick. Returning to Nairobi with the rest of the group, she was undoubtedly anxious about a forthcoming trip to rural Kaimosi, where the students were going to live with Kenyan families for three weeks. How could she function in Kaimosi if she couldn't walk without feeling that the world was spinning around? Then, to make matters worse, another student, Becky, felt sick too.

Sara and her co-leader wondered if they should postpone the trip. Should one of them stay behind? I wasn't teaching yet, and I offered to take the two students to the doctor while the rest of the group departed on the day-long bus ride up-country.

When I called a doctor, I was told to come in right away. The physician worked in a clean office near the British High Commission downtown, seemed careful and competent to me, and put Becky and Elly at ease. "You don't have malaria," he told them authoritatively, and his manner was so persuasive that they believed him at once. Then he prescribed another medication for each woman that he promised would make them feel better soon.

I drove them back to our apartment, and they stretched out on twin beds in our guest room. Sleeping for the better part of the day made a world of difference in their outlook. They were emotionally and physically exhausted. They had landed in Kenya about a month before, gone off to live with Kenyan families in Nairobi for ten days almost immediately on their arrival, and then plunged into an altogether different culture on the coast. As the medicine worked on their symptoms, I thought they benefited almost as much from the time to relax. After another day in Nairobi, they were ready to rejoin their fellow students.

Our Kenyan friends were often not as fortunate. Joy, the seven-year-old daughter of our neighbor Mary, came down with malaria when she was visiting her grandparents in Chuka, in the foothills of Mt. Kenya. The infant son of Eric, an American Studies colleague, likewise had a bout of malaria, even though his parents took full precautions and had him sleep in a crib covered by a mosquito net. Fortunately, both recovered quickly.

But both families—like all our Kenyan friends—had to struggle to get adequate medical care. Such care came with employment at the University of Nairobi, but did not always seem readily accessible. Whenever one of her daughters became sick, Mary had to wait, often for hours, for a clinic doctor to turn up. On occasion, the doctor never showed up. Private care was available, of course, but it was costly.

My student Jeremiah encountered the same problems when he went to get a physical examination prior to coming to the United States. He had been awarded a fellowship to study at Miami University and needed to provide documentation of a number of inoculations. It was difficult enough for him to find a birth certificate. There was no chance of getting a record of any shots, and, indeed, it was unlikely that he had ever had any of the required injections. Jeremiah spent one whole day at the university clinic, waiting for a doctor who never arrived. Finally, I took matters into my own hands, telephoned a physician I knew, and told her I would pay for whatever Jeremiah needed. Access to funds determined the kind of care you could receive.

While we had the money to pay for adequate treatment if the need arose, we still worried about where to go in case of an emergency. Soon after we arrived in the country, Marianne, the cultural attaché at the American Embassy and head of the Fulbright program in Kenya, suggested that we find out how to reach Nairobi Hospital, the best private facility in the city. Much to our relief, it turned out to be only five minutes away. Then, a few months later, Sara and I needed follow-up shots to complete our inoculations against hepatitis. Worried about contaminated needles, we had carried with us a year's supply of disposable syringes. A physician friend told us we could simply go to Nairobi Hospital to get the injections. At the hospital pharmacy, we purchased vials of the serum we needed, then went to an outpatient area, where a doctor gave us the shots (with the hospital's own sterile needles) after but a short wait. The whole process seemed crisp and efficient, perhaps even more so than is often the case in hospitals in the United States.

I felt much less comfortable and less confident, however, when I visited other hospitals in Kenya. In the rural countryside, and even in Nairobi, public hospitals made me cringe. Kenyatta Hospital, in Nairobi, is a huge, sprawling structure, with a relatively new, multistory, block-like building that looks like a castle at the core. Older wards and hallways radiate out from the center, with innumerable ramshackle shacks scattered around the outside. As I wandered through the old section of the hospital on one visit, I was struck by its stark appearance. The walls were painted gray on the bottom, white on the top, with the line between the colors more wavy than straight. Much of the paint was dirty, and the rest was peeling. Some of the ceiling panels were broken, and others had fallen down. Bare lights, some fluorescent, some incandescent, hung from the ceiling, providing a dull and depressing glow. There was a concrete floor. In the tower block, I wandered over to the ward area. In one ward, I noticed a couple of tiny rooms, with a bed shared by two people. I wasn't sure if both were patients. One, I thought, might have been a family member keeping the patient company, or helping ward off evil spirits.

Later, on a visit to Kaimosi, far from the big city, I went over to the local hospital. It was located on the main road into the town, a dirt path barely passable by car. The small building had gray, concrete walls, tinged with red from the iron-impregnated ground. Corrugated metal sheets that had begun to rust covered the roof. The hospital was built around a grassy courtyard, with a number of different wards, each with a dozen beds. Hollow-eyed patients stared from the rooms.

White missionaries had built and staffed the hospital, and for a time it had enjoyed an enviable reputation. When the missionaries finally left, the government took it over, and almost immediately it began to deteriorate, as resources and supplies ended up in private pockets. Now there was not even a doctor on the regular staff. A physician from another district visited from time to time, but most care was provided by nurses and the administrator who was in charge. On the Saturday afternoon when I wandered around, the only nurse on duty was a patient himself, who had risen from his bed and was doing what he could to help others in even worse shape.

Later still, I visited a small clinic in Korogocho, an urban slum in the Nairobi district of Kariobangi, and got a glimpse of the kind of care most Kenyans might receive, if they got any medical attention at all. It was a tiny cement building, with a corrugated metal roof, looking out on a small courtyard surrounded by similar deteriorating structures. The examining area was barely big enough for a patient and a physician, if a doctor was available at all. I watched one consultation done by a day nurse, seated behind his desk as the patient sat on a broken chair. In the next room, there was an eye clinic, and further down the hallway a dental room. The dentist was prepared to do temporary fillings, but not permanent ones, for he lacked a compressor to prepare the necessary mixture. Most frequently he contented himself with extractions, which were easier than filling teeth.

As my stay in Kenya wore on, I became increasingly conscious of the deadly impact of AIDS. All around us, I saw and heard of people dying of AIDS, even when Kenyans neglected to use the Kiswahili term—*ukimwi*—for the disease. If someone had AIDS and died, a friend in Kaimosi told me, it was common to say simply that the person was bewitched.

AIDS in Africa is different than in the United States. We feel the presence of this rampaging epidemic in America, and most people I know at home have relatives, or friends, or friends of friends, who have died from the disease. In the United States alone, the number of deaths from AIDS soared over 250,000 in 1995, and reached 468,000 by the end of 2001. The plague has become part of popular culture. Millions of people saw the powerful film *Philadelphia*, in which Tom Hanks won an Oscar for his portrayal of a gay man dying from the disease. Millions more have helped work on the AIDS quilt, which links together stories and people from all parts of the country. But the impact pales when set against the problems in Africa, where some people speculate the epidemic began.

The first full-fledged cases of AIDS in the region appeared around 1982. By 1997, there were 76,000 cases reported, according to Sobbie Mulindi, a psychiatrist at the University of Nairobi Medical School, who is now vice-chairman of the National AIDS Committee. At the end of 2001, in the latest figures reported by the joint United Nations Programme on HIV/AIDS, there were approximately 2,500,000 Kenyan adults and children—out of a total population of about 30,000,000—living with the virus, whether or not they showed symptoms. An estimated 190,000 Kenyans had already died of the disease. And there were now about 890,000 children under the age of fifteen who had lost at least one parent, and sometimes both, to AIDS.

The disease is most prevalent along the Trans-African Highway. Using the Kiswahili name, Kenyans call this the *Ukimwi* Highway. This road, pock-marked with potholes, is the main truck route in the region. It runs from Mombasa on the Kenyan coast through Nairobi, Nakuru, Eldoret, and finally into Uganda. Far from being an isolated route through rural land, it runs through the major urban centers. All of these areas become vulnerable to the spread of AIDS, transmitted largely by truckers who mingle frequently with prostitutes as they move along. Here, heterosexual contact is the main cause for the spread of the disease.

The prostitution responsible for the unchecked increase in infection is rampant in Nairobi. There was a time, just a few years ago, during my year in Kenya, when people joked that you could always spot the prostitutes, for they were the only women wearing slacks. The city has become more cosmopolitan in the last decade, and that old conservative dress code no longer prevails. But the prostitutes are still easy to find. Some solicit customers along city streets, at all hours of night or day. Others congregate at the clubs, like the Florida 2000 disco or the New Florida nightclub. There, African, European, and American men drink Tusker beer, dance to the throbbing disco beat, and contemplate the inexpensive attractions the women sell.

Once, in the year Sara and I spent in Kenya, we went one evening to the New Florida with a couple of *mzungu* (white) friends from the United States. At first, no one was dancing. Then the women began to dance among themselves. Before long, one man rose and began to move from one woman to another, as if to sample the wares. A couple of other men likewise moved to the floor, dancing mostly with each other, eyeing the women as they brushed by. It wasn't very animated. It didn't seem as though anyone was enjoying the dancing for its own sake. But there was a good deal of looking around.

When Kip, Sara's language teacher, took us to the notorious bar known as the Modern Green, we had a chance to watch the local prostitutes at even closer hand. As we nursed our beer, we bantered with the women as they approached our table, then moved on after ascertaining our lack of interest. At one point, when I needed to go out to a restroom, I found several prostitutes talking among themselves in front of the door. Once again, they wanted to laugh and joke together, particularly at the expense of a *mzungu* from America, before moving away to let me get inside. I found myself caught up in a kind of morbid fascination at the chaotic scene. I felt vaguely awkward, eager to use my Kiswahili, but reluctant to get too involved.

Along the coast, the prostitution is even more visible, and, here, both men and women ply their trade. Beach boys roam near the tourist hotels in Mombasa, Malindi, and Lamu, preying on white women from Europe and America eager for a good time. Each time we left Lamu, we watched the beach boys, usually with dreadlocks, accompany the latest trophy to the airport to say goodbye. Lamu is a tiny place, and the odds were we had seen the particular couple over the course of the past few days, at a variety of restaurants and juice bars, or in the gift shops or henna parlors where women could have their hands or feet painted in patterns favored by Kenya's Islamic women. Seeing the female tourists and their beach boys interact in often stiff ways as these one- or two- or three-night stands came to an end, I worried about the long-term consequences of the possible exposure to AIDS.

A number of Kenyan customs also contribute to the spread of AIDS. In a culture where polygamy still exists, the disease moves quickly through multiple families with devastating results. Among some ethnic groups, the widow of a man who dies is expected to marry the dead man's next eldest brother. In the past, this gave the woman protection and kept property in family hands. But if the first husband died of AIDS and the wife was exposed, this custom provides one more avenue for the disease to continue to spread.

Sara worried about her American students at those times when they went out for an evening of fun in Nairobi. They loved to drink and to dance, and the discos drew them in. But the warnings about the likelihood of infection were loud and clear, from the first orientation session in Indiana to the end of their Kenyan stay. "No sex!" she said. "You can't afford to take the chance with the rest of your life." It's not always easy to get that message across to a group of college students accustomed to expressing their sexuality in whatever ways they choose. But in this case, the stakes were too high to fool around, and they heeded her words.

The Kenyan government is now concerned about the scourge, although it seemed indifferent when AIDS first burst onto the scene. Officials worried, then, that the country might lose tourist revenue and other foreign aid if word of the epidemic got out, and so it made strenuous efforts to avoid acknowledging or discussing the disease. At the same time, it tried to curtail the efforts of aid agencies and international health experts to intervene. Later, it appointed a committee to look into the problem. In Kenya, as elsewhere, forming a committee is often a way of indicating that action is being taken, even if nothing is ever done. In this case, the government incorporated a National AIDS Control Committee into the Ministry of Health, then dismissed representatives from nongovernmental organizations. Eventually, foreign donors insisted they be reinstated and began to exert pressure on the government to take more aggressive action to try to curtail the spread of the epidemic. Even so, the mandate for the Control Committee remained a cautious one. The development plan for the 1989-1993 period stated: "To the extent that AIDS has become an issue of international concern, the Committee will work closely with relevant regional and international agencies to control the spread of AIDS and in furthering research on its possible cure."

In the last decade, Kenya has finally accepted the need to take aggressive actions to contain the disease. As you travel along the nation's highways, you can see signs warning men—and women—to keep their sexual activities within the framework of their families. Most of the small billboards are aimed at an audience whose literacy may be in doubt. They contain simple images—sometimes even stick figures—of men, women, and children in a family setting, along with relatively brief captions telling people to use condoms.

On one visit to Kenyatta Hospital, I came across a hallway with a number of AIDS posters. One showed three huts in the upper right corner, with a group of people gathered together under a tree on the left. A caption at the top read: "DON'T BE FOOLED. AIDS IS NOT WITCHCRAFT. AIDS IS REAL." Another caption at the bottom counseled: "AVOID SEX BEFORE MARRIAGE. STICK TO ONE PARTNER OR USE A CONDOM." I found another poster, called the "Secret Lovers Club," in a different part of the hospital. It showed a group of women on the left, carrying red, heart-shaped handbags. A group of men stood on the right. As you moved further away from a door at the top, the figures became more and more skeleton-like, until they were mere corpses at the bottom. The caption read: "AIDS KILLS. Use condoms."

The condom campaign has become intensive. Foreign-aid agencies dispense condoms free of charge. Yet it often seems that the campaign falls on deaf ears. As I walked daily along Nairobi streets in 1995, I frequently came across piles of condoms, unused and still in cellophane packets, discarded on the sidewalk or by the side of the road. These had likely been provided free of charge and then thrown away.

Resistance to condoms comes from a variety of fronts. The country is made up of a series of ethnic groups—the Kikuyu, the Luo, the Luyha, the Kalenjin, and many more—and rivalries, deep-rooted and often promoted by the government in the 1990s to maintain its own political power, remain very much alive. Such groups, caught in contentious quarrels, have traditionally frowned on contraception. As newspaper correspondent Blaine Harden once noted, "Family planning officials have found that no tribe wants to be the one that stops growing first."

Kenyan sexual customs also contribute to the unwillingness to use condoms. "Cultural upbringing makes it impossible for women to negotiate," Leah

Wanjama, a Kenyan gender researcher, observed in early 1996. "The dilemma most women face is that if they suggest the use of a condom, their partner will think they have been having affairs or are suspicious of them." Men resist for other reasons as well. In 1996, Sara and I heard Arthur Obel, a government physician engaged in AIDS research, deliver a lecture about his work. Commenting on why he believed that condoms would never work, he proclaimed proudly, "Kenyan men will never stand for them. They like skin-to-skin." And then he made an openly sexual gesture with both hands to illustrate what he had in mind. Obel was also allegedly responsible for an outrageous story, spread in Nairobi's newspapers, about condoms laced with the AIDS virus that had been contributed by foreign nations as a way of trying to weaken Kenya and other African countries in the competition for global power.

Today, condoms are becoming more acceptable. The countryside is filled with billboards advertising the Trust brand. In one configuration, a couple appears in silhouette form, with the caption "Let's Talk." In another, a Trust condom is visible among other belongings with the Kiswahili caption reading, "*Una yako?*" — "Do you have yours?"

Some Kenyans have also been active in the effort to find a cure for AIDS. More than a decade ago, local scientists developed a drug known as Kemron to heal those suffering from the disease. The remedy soon proved to be ineffective. Then, in March 1996, Obel produced a concoction called Pearl Omega. It was, he said, a protease inhibitor, and he announced that he had successfully reversed the course of seven HIV-positive patients, who now tested negative after taking the drug.

Obel was a showman. When Sara and I heard him speak at the United Kenya Club, he proudly presented a container of Pearl Omega, packaged in what looked like a wine bottle, to the Chairman of the Club. He also used his government connections to advance his own ends. Because he was employed in the Office of the President, a key location in this authoritarian, highly-centralized state, he had tremendous political support. Indeed, soon after the appearance of the new drug, the government announced that it cured AIDS, *before* scientists in Kenya or elsewhere in the world had been able to conduct independent tests of their own.

A comical national debate about the efficacy of Pearl Omega followed. The press charged that the reason Obel had such substantial government support was that he was secretly treating a sizable number of prominent, highly-placed officials, who had tremendous political clout. Finally, as a number of patients whom he had claimed to have made "HIV negative" took him to court, charging the so-called cure did not work, the government bowed to scientific pressure and banned the drug. Ironically, these actions occurred as scientists in other parts of the world were proposing a cocktail of drugs, including protease inhibitors, that could be used to slow, or sometimes to reverse, the course of AIDS. But those concoctions were being tested in public, controlled trials that produced results other researchers could replicate and thus had a credibility altogether lacking in the Kenyan case.

Obel is not the only AIDS researcher in Kenya. Other more reputable scientists and physicians are involved in the effort to deal with the dread disease, but their activities are less visible and they usually receive less publicity.

Illness, as horrendous as it tends to be here, is but one cause of death in Kenya. Random violence, particularly in the urban regions, likewise takes its toll. Each week, the *Nation* and other newspapers contain stories about the constant muggings and car-jackings—and their often lethal results. Not even ambassadors or other highly-placed officials are safe. Break-ins continue to occur with a depressing regularity, even at residences with electronic alarm systems and armed guards posted all around. One British diplomat, during my year at the University of Nairobi, tried to elude car-jackers intent on stealing his four-wheel-drive vehicle as he was returning to his home in Nairobi. He took a bullet in the spine that left him paralyzed from the waist down, and finally killed him when he returned to Britain for surgery to ease his pain.

Though theft is widespread, Kenyans become furious when it occurs, and respond with a kind of vigilante justice, just like crowds in the old American West. We read vivid accounts of would-be robbers who were captured and sometimes killed by angry crowds. In one such story, an unfortunate Kenyan government official came out of his office and tried to unlock his car. Unfortunately, he approached the wrong vehicle, easy to do since virtually every car seems to be a white Peugeot or Nissan or Toyota with similar dents. Car alarms are a requirement for registration, and when the official tried to jiggle the lock, which failed to respond to the wrong key, the alarm began to wail. A crowd gathered around and threatened to dismember him before he realized his mistake and was able to escape and get to the correct car.

Not all violent episodes, however, occur in the cities. Midway through my stay in Kenya, a group of Japanese tourists in a safari van on the road to the famous game park Masai Mara were attacked by bandits. They lost all their belongings after a gunfight that left them terrified but still alive.

Julie Ward, an English journalist camping in Masai Mara in 1990, was less lucky. She had ventured into the park in her own vehicle, and remained there by herself when her companion returned to Nairobi. For reasons that still remain unclear, she was attacked, killed, and dismembered, and her body was burned beyond recognition. The government claimed that bandits were responsible. Critics charged that she may have stumbled upon a government-endorsed smuggling operation. The chief warden of the national park was almost immediately reassigned to another post in Nairobi, and a superficial investigation found nothing untoward. Yet the case refused to die, as Ward's father insisted on a better explanation and pursued justice with a tiger-like tenacity. For years, the case continued to surface occasionally. As I prepared to leave Kenya after spending the summer of 1997 there, the case was in the news once more, but still not fully resolved.

Meanwhile, the roads themselves lead to innumerable equally grisly deaths. We bought a car in 1995, figuring that we would be as safe in our own vehicle as in any of the buses or *matatus*—brightly colored minivans, with music blaring from open windows—that carry passengers all over Kenya. The *matatus* all had names, like Twister, Comet, Shooting Star, and best of all, Hippo of the Road. Usually hauling twenty passengers on seats built for ten, the *matatus* were always in a hurry, speeding through the streets with a kind of devil-may-care attitude in the search for a few extra passengers and the fares they would bring. The vehicles themselves usually needed repair, as owners cut corners in the constant effort to save as much money as they could. Sometimes brakes failed. More often, the driver took a turn too quickly and found himself turning over or careening into a ditch. We passed such accidents every time we went out in the car, and took to giving the buses and *matatus* as wide a berth as we could.

The heavily rutted roads contribute to what the *Nation* graphically calls "road carnage." Drivers swerving to avoid gaping holes in both small alleys and main thoroughfares sometimes head straight for oncoming cars. Defensive driving means getting out of the way.

Passing remains another cause of carnage. There is only one highway with double lanes in the country. For the most part, two-lane roads are the norm. Trucks, usually with limited power, labor loudly as they slow down when climbing even small inclines. A line of cars, often ten or fifteen long, follows, as the vehicles snake their way around scores of blind turns. Eventually, one driver becomes impatient and passes the cars and trucks in front, hoping, but never knowing, that there is no vehicle coming in the opposite direction. We watched an almost unimaginable number of close calls. We also saw several cars crash.

Roundabouts, what New Englanders call rotaries, are equally dangerous. Drivers whip around these circular intersections, located along Uhuru Highway and in other congested areas of Nairobi, before spinning off on the side street of their choice. Cars are expected to follow a certain vehicular etiquette. Those in the outside lane are supposed to turn off to the left, though, as often as not, they might go straight. Those in the center lane are expected to continue on that way, though they might turn in any direction. Those in the right lane might make a turn at the street three-quarters of the way around the circle, or continue straight. There was, one police chief told me, a book of regulations, but after looking all over Nairobi, we found that no one could produce a copy. And accidents occurred in the roundabouts all the time.

The roads remain equally dangerous for pedestrians, who often walk along highways or simply need to cross a road. A few intersections have traffic lights, but those are frequently out-of-order and even more commonly ignored. You can wait for the light to change, but still need to look carefully as you make your way across the street.

People we knew died on the roads with depressing regularity during our year in Kenya. Soon after we arrived, we read about the death of distinguished Kenyan historian Gideon Were in a *matatu* accident. Not long after, the chairman of the University Council was killed in a crash as he was going to his up-country home. A friend who was headmaster of a prominent boarding school likewise died in a car crash. Another good friend, an internationally renowned philosopher named Odera Oruka, died when he was hit by a truck while crossing the street. He had given a guest lecture to Sara's American students just a week before the accident ended his life.

Oruka's death gave us some sense of the Kenyan traditions surrounding human loss. He was a Luo, and the Luos take their burial customs very seriously. Oruka's eldest son, a student in the United States, was summoned home to participate in the funeral and to help the family cope with the loss. We visited the family house in a prosperous section of Nairobi, and found dozens, even hundreds, of people gathered together at different times. We observed the talking, singing, even wailing on occasion, before people made the journey to the up-country village that was really Oruka's home. There, the huge burial party bade farewell to the body while placating the ancestral spirits that would keep watch in years to come.

Different groups treat death differently. Some Luhya friends up-country in the Kaimosi area bury their dead in front of their homes. The Meru people near Mt. Kenya used to leave a body in the woods, to be consumed by animals. But all groups treat the dead with a profound respect, far more intense than anything we had ever seen back home.

Sickness and death, often the result of poor or nonexistent medical care, offer a depressing glimpse at the underside of Kenyan life. The colorful customs we came to appreciate, both in Nairobi and in rural areas as well, could not hide the all-too-common confrontations with sickness and death that we saw all around. When Mary came to tell us about her young niece's death, she was matter-of-fact about the loss. She, and all our Kenyan friends, valued human life as much as we did, yet treated illness as unavoidable and regarded death with a kind of fatalism that may have been a larger part of American culture a century ago, but has now disappeared. We *expect* to get better when we are ill. In Africa, it is hard to be as confident about overcoming disease. I worried about our friends and their ailments that should have been routine and, each time they became ill, I hoped desperately they would survive.

The Politics of Fear

In Kenya, as in most of Africa, everything has a price. You can find anything, or arrange anything, as long as you provide the requisite cash. The business world has long operated according to such patterns; now the political realm functions the same way. In all parts of the world, politics means exploring the limits of the possible and finding ways to make things work. Sometimes that involves greasing the bureaucratic wheels to gain necessary support, but the costs of such lubrication can be high.

Every transaction in Kenya—legal, commercial, or political—has its cost. Sometimes the request comes quietly, and money passes without comment from one pocket to the next. More often, the solicitation is blatant and bold. Sometimes the amount demanded is minuscule; occasionally the price can be sky-high. But the basic principle is the same: Money changes hands.

Kenyans are fond of talking about *kitu kidogo*, the Kiswahili phrase for "a little thing." People joke that the best advice about how to get anything done is *"Toa kitu kidogo,"* which is, quite simply, an injunction to give a little something. For linguistic variety, they also speak of such a lubricant as *chai*, or "tea."

I first encountered *kitu kidogo* when the telephone repairman came to my home to find out why the phone didn't work. As he considered wiring my fax machine to the main line, he knew he should ask permission from his head office first. "I help you, and you help me," he said in halting English, and I just smiled ingenuously, not comprehending what he meant. I realized later what he was asking for, but by then it was too late. Instead of accommodating his request, I got him a Phillips screwdriver, offered him a soft drink, and thanked him as effusively as I could for helping with the phone. Unlike some people I encountered in the year that followed, he was gracious, and overlooked my innocent, but unwelcome, response without compromising the task at hand.

Over the course of the next year, friend after friend filled me in about how the system worked. Justus, my taxi-driver confidant, complained about trying to get a telephone line extended to the house he had built the year before. He filled out the necessary application, and provided the government power office with a detailed map showing how to reach his plot of land. Months later, he received a form letter informing him that officials could not find the plot. That was absurd, I agreed. Even I had been able to reach his house the first time I went out there, and I didn't even have a map. It was a clear case of harassment, as a clerk somewhere in the bureaucracy sought a bribe.

Sometimes the request is even more transparent. Donald, an English friend who has lived in Kenya for the past forty years, wanted to build an extension onto his house, and needed approval of his plans from the city council before he could proceed with construction. He had to pay a fee of 15,000 Kenya shillings (about $200) simply to have an inspector come out to the house, look at the property, and examine the plans. That payment was above board and listed in the instructions about how to proceed. But when Donald picked the inspector up to drive him to the site, the official began talking about the bribes other people had paid to make sure they got the necessary service. Ten thousand shillings was the going price, he said. Donald politely demurred. Back at the house, after the examination had taken place, they drank coffee and talked for an hour. When Donald finally said that he had better drive the official back to town, the forlorn inspector asked, "Can't you even manage 2,000 shillings?" to which Donald replied that he neither took nor accepted bribes. Plan approval did not come until Donald found a former student working in the main planning office who was willing to expedite the process, out of friendship, with no payment at all.

Mary, our neighbor and friend, provided the best explanation of how the system worked. "You cannot get a lot of things moving in the public offices unless you pay something small," she said. "A file gets lost, or is misplaced, but once you pay something small, the file will be there within the next two minutes." She told about going into an office and being told that the person who needed to sign a check she was supposed to pick up was not there. Then the clerk to whom she was talking told her that if she gave a little something, he could find the person. In this transaction, as in so many others, Mary said with a smile, it turned out that "the same person you were talking to early on happens to be the one with the pen."

A frightening encounter with *kitu kidogo* came when I was on the road. On one occasion, a policeman on the outskirts of the city flagged me down and told me I was exceeding the speed limit of fifty miles per hour. I would have to go to court the next day, he said. Or I could settle the matter then and there. He wrote a figure on a piece of paper—6,000 Kenya shillings, which was over $100. That was exorbitant, even by American standards. I gasped.

I knew that I had not been speeding and that he was testing me. I looked for a radar gun. There was none, of course. There was no radar gun in the whole country. "I couldn't possibly have been going that fast," I said. "Cars were passing me, and my car vibrates at that speed."

My answer made no difference. The policeman circled the number he had drawn on his pad.

At that point, I switched into Kiswahili, hoping it would help. It did no good.

Almost at my wit's end, I decided to call his bluff. I said, "Let me write down your name and badge number, so when I go to court I can tell the judge what's been going on."

That ploy worked. The policeman looked at me a long time, then said, in Kiswahili, "*Potea*"—"Get lost."

I should have learned the lesson that I was lucky to have escaped serious trouble in a police state, but I forgot all about the episode. Then, a few months later, I found myself in the midst of an even more terrifying confrontation. I was evidently in the wrong lane in a roundabout in downtown Nairobi, and a number of other drivers blared their horns in anger. As the traffic signal turned red, I made another blunder: I stopped at the light. A policeman, dealing with a wholly unrelated accident at the site, came over to my car. "*Umefanya makosa*," he said in Kiswahili. "You made a mistake." Then, like the other policeman, he said, "You can go to court, or you can settle it here."

I tried to call his bluff, as I had with the other official. Hoping he would drop the matter, I said, "I'll go to court." That was my second mistake.

"In that case," the policeman said, "we're going to the police station." He got into my car and said "*Twende.*" "Let's go." Once there, he asked me if I had enough money to post a bond. If not, he said, he would have to impound my car.

I began to realize I was in over my head as I was called before the police chief. I tried to speak Kiswahili, but he shrugged me off in fluent, grammatical English that made my linguistic efforts look lame. At that point, I began to apologize profusely for the errors of my ways. Thumbing through my license, registration, passport, and work permit, he seemed to soften and said to the policeman who had apprehended me, "I think we'll give him a warning this time, if it's all right with you." The policeman, ever respectful of authority, nodded and I breathed a sigh of relief. I was free again, but found myself wondering whether a little *kitu kidogo* would have been easier all around.

The problem was that the system affected the entire country and, sometimes, turned into *kitu kubwa*—a big thing—which involved monumental graft. A case in point was the effort to repair the Nairobi-Mombasa Road, part of the Trans-African Highway bisecting both the country and the continent.

While I was in Kenya, this road was a disaster, the site of countless accidents for years. In some places, the road had eroded so badly that the pavement was barely wide enough for a single car. If a truck happened to be heading toward you in the oncoming lane, you had no choice but to get off the road to avoid a fatal crash. Finally, recognizing the tremendous cost to commerce, the World Bank helped arrange financing for a massive repair project. The Bank wanted a single contractor and, given the size of the project, such a company would undoubtedly have had to come from abroad. The Kenyan government insisted that the project be broken down into several component parts, so that local companies could bid on and win the contracts for the road. Given the state of local road-building, the inevitable award to Kenyan firms probably compromised the integrity of the final result, but the World Bank agreed, since it is important to try to promote local autonomy whenever possible. In time, the process got underway, with corruption inevitably involved, including bidding by some companies that did not actually exist, but could nonetheless reap the profits of the project. "Pretty common stuff," a friend at the World Bank remarked. A year later, the rehabilitation of the road had barely begun.

A far more serious problem was the Goldenberg scandal that rocked the country in the 1990s and continues to be an embarrassment today. I remember having been appalled when I learned that Boss Tweed, the American political boss in mid-nineteenth century New York, and his associates had pocketed a small fortune when a courthouse expected to cost $250,000 ended up requiring $8,000,000, even before the building was done. What I saw in Kenya made those antics 150 years ago seem insignificant by comparison. The Goldenberg affair began when the government decided to provide a subsidy to promote exports that brought hard currency into the country. If an exporter could prove that an item had been sold and exported for American dollars or German marks or English pounds, the merchant would receive an incentive subsidy paid in shillings. To receive the subsidy, a company had to show bank transfers to demonstrate that hard currency had really changed hands.

Taking advantage of this incentive, a wealthy entrepreneur named Kamlesh Pattni embarked on a scheme to export gold to obtain the subsidy in local currency. A company, given the fictitious name Goldenberg, was formed to export what turned out to be nonexistent gold. Further compounding the deception, customs agents involved in the plot stamped the necessary papers to confirm that the fraudulent export was indeed taking place. As if that was not enough, the Minister of Finance added an additional percentage to the original subsidy, to ensure that everyone involved could profit even more fully from the corrupt scheme.

To show that hard currency had entered the country, Pattni and his associates cut more corners. Instead of showing bank drafts, as required by law, they provided government authorities with deposit slips, which were accepted by the officials in charge. But these simply reflected the actions of wily entrepreneurs borrowing all kinds of hard currency from black marketeers on the street, making a deposit in their own account, and then returning the suitcases of cash to the original source in return for a modest fee.

Eventually the entrepreneurs overreached themselves. The scam became public and generated a mounting sense of outrage. The *Nation* engaged in some able and energetic investigative reporting and described the scandal in detailed terms. Pattni and his associates were indicted and faced more than ninety separate charges.

But neither exposure nor indictment was enough to put the scoundrels away. Judgeships are political appointments, and judges serve at the pleasure of the president. The government, at least until recently, rhetorically affirmed the value of an independent judiciary, but, in fact, made sure that judges did what was necessary for top officials to retain their stranglehold over the country. In this case, with highly placed politicians implicated in the scheme, the judiciary responded appropriately, from the government's point of view. After a suitable interval, the judge hearing the case agreed with a defense motion that there were too many different charges—and then dropped the case altogether. Apparently, other alternatives were not entertained. As outrage mounted in Kenya, and, more importantly, in the donor community outside, pressure to let justice take its course began to mount. The International Monetary Fund held up a forthcoming loan and prompted the Attorney General, another political appointee, to call for three new charges to be filed, but even then it was not clear just what would happen next. Referring to the entire scandal, a friend observed that "basically, it's just another way of transferring public resources into private pockets." The only problem was that, this time, the transfer of funds involved in the Goldenberg affair had come close to the total amount of money provided to Kenya by both the World Bank and the International Monetary Fund over a period of several years.

Today, a decade after the inception of the Goldenberg scheme, a new government has established a commission to make public the dimensions of the scam. In hearings that are published regularly in the press, the appalling fact has emerged that the perpetrators bilked the Kenyan people out of billions of shillings, amounting at the very least to hundreds of millions of dollars.

As I returned to Kenya again and again, I came to realize how the all-pervasive corruption, which affects both private and public life, was slowly eroding stability, security, and confidence in the government. People in the 1990s recognized the need for change, but most acknowledged that the current regime was unwilling, and probably unable, to root out the decay. Protest riots became far more frequent in Kenya—culminating in the formation of a new government at the end of 2002.

As a historian, I wondered both where the corruption had come from and how Kenya, once viewed by the outside world as the bright light of Africa, had fallen on such hard times. The answer, I slowly discovered in conversations with colleagues at the university, Godfrey in particular, and in the books I read, is rooted in the larger political patterns that developed in the years since independence was gained in 1963. Strong and ruthless leaders, eager to consolidate their own power at all costs, built upon the example of the British rulers earlier in the century, who had used their considerable resources to suppress dissent. One autocrat after another has drawn skillfully on the lessons of the colonial past and used the patterns of repression devised then to secure personal and political advantage in the post-independence years, all with the moral and financial support of the Western world, in exchange for loyalty in the midst of the Cold War.

The British in Kenya, as elsewhere in the empire, had been concerned with advancing their own interests, with little concern for their colonial subjects. As they consolidated their power in Kenya in the years after 1895, they relegated the Africans who had long inhabited the country to subservient roles. They seized land held both by ethnic groups and by individuals, and began to cultivate it themselves. The White Highlands, as the region north of Nairobi came to be called, fell firmly under British control. Taxes on the huts they lived in forced the Africans who had been evicted from their lands to work for their colonial masters to earn the necessary funds. As a nationalist protest movement began to develop in the 1920s, the British outlawed political parties and began to play one group against another in an effort to prevent the Kenyans from uniting in a way that might help them achieve their revolutionary demands.

Colonial authority became even more repressive in the early 1950s, when the Mau Mau rebellion, led by Kikuyu, Meru, and Embu activists, threatened to undermine British control of the country. Mau Mau warriors threw the colonial power into a state of panic. Unsure when the freedom fighters might strike next, the British responded by imposing a state of emergency on the entire country. Restrictive measures outlawed criticism of the government and assembly without a permit. Nationalist leaders found themselves detained. In the end, Great Britain ended the rebellion, but failed to squelch the larger drive for independence, which came just a few years later. Yet the new constitution heralding the shift in power still contained the harsh provisions the British had promulgated in their effort to head off the drive for freedom.

Jomo Kenyatta, the Kikuyu hero of the struggle for independence who became the new republic's first president, moved aggressively to consolidate his own power. He is still a hero in Kenya today. There is a Kenyatta Conference Center, a Kenyatta University, and a Kenyatta Avenue in Nairobi. People think of Kenyatta as the father of his country, just as we consider George Washington the father of ours. But the adulation for, and obsequiousness to, political leaders is far more pronounced in Kenya than in the United States. Perhaps, I began to realize, the unrestricted exercise of power is necessary to create required political support in a time of transition. But even then, it often seemed to go too far.

The ideas Kenyatta advanced remain influential today. He popularized the notion of *harambee*—working together—to create a sense of national cohesion. People joined together with one another to build schools and other institutions needed by the fledgling state. Meanwhile, he preserved his own power by deftly foiling his opponents. In the first years of freedom, he put down a Somali-aided guerrilla rebellion on the northeastern border and quelled an army uprising in Nairobi with the help of British forces. He then improved conditions for enlisted men and promoted Kenyans into positions held by white expatriates in the past. He also infiltrated the military services with members of his own intelligence team.

At the same time, he strengthened his political command. When Vice President Oginga Odinga, a Luo from the Lake Victoria region in the west, proclaimed "Communism is like food to me," Kenyatta responded by publicly taking an anti-communist stance, which earned him the gratitude and support of the West. Though Odinga had been an ally in the independence struggle, he now became a political enemy who lost power in a Cabinet shuffle aimed at moving him out. Eventually, in 1966, Odinga resigned from KANU, Kenyatta's party, and formed an opposition party of his own. After allowing opposition for a time, Kenyatta arrested and detained its leaders, disqualified other recalcitrant members from running for Parliament by claiming they had filled out registration forms improperly, and then denied them a presence in the legislative chamber by declaring that they had won an insufficient number of parliamentary seats. Kenya was now effectively a one-party state.

Kenyatta today looms larger than life. The elaborate mausoleum next to Parliament in Nairobi testifies to the powerful impact he had on the country. But the memorial says nothing about the techniques responsible for his success. Kenyatta was a master tactician, a politician who could be rigid one moment, flexible the next, ruthlessly willing to do whatever suited his purposes in the end. Ruling through his Kikuyu compatriots, as the British had done, he marginalized his opponents and made sure they posed no threat. His firm domination of the civil service established his bureaucratic and administrative control. Through all of this, though, he remained popular with the people, who called him *Mzee*, or Elder, and treated him with affection and respect.

In newly independent Kenya, an informal underground system of nepotism and patronage favoring the Kikuyu became increasingly important. At some levels, this led to extortion and theft. A dozen years into his tenure as president, Kenyatta's wife Mama Ngina and other members of his family were accused of gouging the public and profiteering for private gain. Mama Ngina was denounced for her involvement with ivory poaching and with the destruction of delicate ecosystems in the process of making charcoal to sell to the Arabian Gulf. Then, as now, the charges failed to result in any fundamental change. More and more, the nation began to suffer from increasing disparities, like those in colonial times, between the relatively few wealthy Kenyans and the masses who had virtually nothing. In the past, the British had been the wealthy masters. Now rich and powerful Kenyans themselves took over that role.

Meanwhile, Kenya fell prey to the politics of assassination. Politicians who appeared to pose too much of a threat often ended up dead. Tom Mboya was the best-known of those murdered. A Luo like Odinga, Mboya had emerged as one of Kenyatta's closest political allies. He served as head of the government's Planning Ministry and as secretary-general of Kenyatta's political party. His trade union activities provided him with considerable support, both at home and abroad, and his organizational and persuasive abilities brought him to the attention of the West. He was the kind of flamboyant and articulate politician prized by the Kennedy administration in the United States, a man whose popular appeal matched John Kennedy's own charismatic charm. As Kenyatta's health faltered in the years after independence, attention focused on Mboya as a possible successor to the *Mzee*. But Kikuyu politicians began to fear the passage of power to a non-Kikuyu, and a fierce power struggle broke out. Mboya's ability to transcend ethnic and tribal boundaries only made him more of a threat. In mid-1969, as he left a shop in Nairobi after doing a routine errand, an African assassin gunned him down. Riots in Luoland, and elsewhere, rocked the country. Kenyatta contained the discontent and continued to consolidate Kikuyu power, but at a growing cost.

In much the same way, Josiah Mwangi Kariuki ran afoul of authorities. A Kikuyu member of Parliament who had once been a prominent member of the administration, he became leader of an unofficial opposition group and challenged the clique surrounding Kenyatta. With a sizable following of the poor and helpless, he demanded political and social change to create a more egalitarian state. In early 1975, police officers abducted him from a Nairobi hotel. When his lifeless body was finally found, circumstances suggested a cover-up on the part of the government, a conclusion supported by a parliamentary commission report. Kenyatta responded with a brutal display of unbridled power, punishing, purging, and detaining his political enemies and silencing the threat for a time.

That pattern of control persisted in the regime of Daniel arap Moi, who became president when Kenyatta died in 1978. Moi followed in Kenyatta's footsteps, and in the footsteps of many other African leaders, by building up the nation while exploiting it at the same time. In the process, Kenya became even more centralized, and more repressive, than it was in Kenyatta's day.

Like my Kenyan friends, I became preoccupied with conversations about politics, in general, and the president, in particular. I listened to all speculation, recounted the stories I heard, and participated in the political discussion that made all of us feel involved—without any access or awareness of what was really going on.

In the process, though, I learned a good deal about how Kenya's second president became so strong. Moi learned his lessons well as he quietly consolidated his own power base in the Kenyatta years. He recognized the realities of Kenyan political life and determined to do what was necessary to rule once he had the chance. Kenyatta had ruled through a Kikuyu clique, which caused serious resentment on the part of those who found themselves outside the inner circle. Moi belonged to the much smaller Kalenjin group and, over the course of the two decades after he assumed power, he systematically promoted his own ethnic associates and their close neighbors at the expense of the Kikuyus and their allies. More important, he marginalized and destroyed his political enemies even more ruthlessly than Kenyatta had done. While we in the West read in our newspapers—if only infrequently—about the struggles that threaten to destabilize Kenya and prevent it from developing economically, the real story is more complicated than it appears in these superficial accounts. Moi, I learned from my African friends, was responsible for exacerbating ethnic rivalries for his own purposes in a pattern that follows the actions of the British almost a century ago. He also encouraged ethnic clashes at election time to provide an excuse to undermine and uproot political rivals in the ostensible interest of national stability.

As vice president, Moi automatically became president for three months after Kenyatta's death. In that brief period, he demonstrated the political skill and the capacity for intrigue that kept him in power for nearly twenty-five years. Working closely with some of the Kikuyu elders, among them Attorney General Charles Njonjo, he persuaded his enemies that he posed no threat and gained their support in winning the election that soon took place. In the years that followed, he spoke incessantly about *nyayo*—following in his predecessor's footsteps—as he sought to make Kenyatta's mandate his own. For a short time, he sought to end factionalism and promote a more unified state. He released political detainees in an attempt to create good will, and spoke out publicly against corruption that was undermining the nation's economic health. But economic decline, in the face of one of the highest rate of population

growth in the world, hindered his efforts and Kenya continued to face difficulties that Moi would not or could not overcome.

Then, in 1982, an attempted coup d'état ended the campaign to create good
will once and for all. In the middle of one quiet August night, air force per-
sonnel seized the national radio station just a block away from the University
of Nairobi and proclaimed that "rampant corruption and nepotism have made
life almost intolerable in our society." At dawn, loyal army troops counterat-
tacked and, by noon, the rebellion was over. Moi disbanded the air force, arrested the rebels the army could find, and embarked on a campaign of repression to maintain his political control that never ended.

I found myself fascinated by the bald but effective efforts at self-promotion.
Like many other African leaders, Moi crafted an all-powerful image in a sys-
tematic campaign to demonstrate that he was the heart and soul of the state. All
money—every coin and every bill—contained his image. All shops, restaurants,
hotels, and commercial establishments posted his picture on a wall, as the photographs of his predecessor were long since laid aside. As American journalist
Richard Reeves wrote in the *Baltimore Sun* in mid-1985, when the process was
still young, Moi "seems determined to eliminate free speech and simplify map-
making by naming everything in the country after himself." A massive monu-
ment in downtown Nairobi, built to commemorate his first ten years in power,
featured his arm holding his trademark *rungu*, a small silver- and ivory-inlaid
mace. It is perhaps symbolic that the testimonial fell into a serious state of disrepair and was mocked or ignored by most people who passed by, but even today, with Moi out of power, it still dominates the corner on which it stands.

Every evening in the Moi years, the television news began with a story
hailing the latest exploits of "His Excellency the President Daniel arap Moi,"
regardless of whatever important events may have taken place either in
Kenya or elsewhere in the world. In Kenya, under Moi, there was one, and
only one, president. An organization could have a chairman, or a chief, but
not a president. When this megalomaniacal policy took effect, the Nairobi
Hebrew Congregation to which I belonged began calling its leader the *Rosh
Kahilah*, Hebrew for head of the community.

At first, I found myself amused by the image-making. But the more it came
to seem inescapable, the more uncomfortable I became. I felt myself caught
up in this carefully cultivated charade, wondering whether a different political reality could ever be possible than the one being crafted before my eyes.

I had to give Moi grudging respect for the support he demanded and received, just as I had reluctantly applauded Lyndon Johnson when he imposed
his own will on the United States in the mid-1960s. "I would like ministers,
assistant ministers, and others to sing like a parrot after me," Moi said in
1984, in a statement that rang true to the end of his tenure. Because Kenyan

officials needed the presidential blessing to be able to accomplish anything at all in the country, they engaged in fawning and obsequious praise that conditioned all public debate. As *Washington Post* correspondent Blaine Hardin commented on such sycophancy, "No speech is complete without flowery mention of the president's Solomon-like wisdom, his astute economic policies, his penetrating analysis of foreign affairs, his love of small children." Vice President Josephat Karanja, for example, hailed Moi's "unrivaled" statesmanship and "unswerving loyalty for institutions nurtured since independence" in a parliamentary address in 1989, and then concluded by declaring that "his warm, passionate heart . . . his deep love for Kenyans, especially the youth, and his genuine patriotism make President Moi the most popular leader in the world." Such orchestrated adulation, when coupled with absolute control over the military and the police, allowed Moi to do whatever he wanted.

One source of strength was Moi's remarkable ability to keep the people around him off guard. Hardin reported a private conversation with a member of Parliament in which Moi explained how he stroked and silenced his subordinates: "You know a balloon is a very small thing. But I can pump it up to such an extent that it will be big and look very important. All you need to make it small again is to prick it with a needle." Staff members, assistants, and even members of his cabinet knew the president could prick the balloon he inflated at any time.

I watched the process unfold for one ill-fated assistant while I taught at the University of Nairobi. Philip Mbithi had served as vice chancellor of the university some years before and had been rewarded for his strong rule of the institution by appointment as the president's chief of staff. As the official responsible for the government bureaucracy, he enjoyed enormous power and full access to the president himself. But Mbithi performed his duties with an arrogance that made unnecessary enemies, and eventually they brought him down. When the president finally decided Mbithi was expendable and appointed him to a position in Tanzania that amounted to a kind of political exile, he refused to leave gracefully. Declining the new appointment, he committed the unpardonable sin of challenging the president publicly. Almost immediately, he found himself out of office, facing a huge tax bill on lands that had been a presidential gift. Some of my Kenyan friends worried about possible threats on his life.

Other top officials faced similar problems. Just a month after Vice President Karanja's fulsome performance in Parliament, singing the president's praises in such extravagant terms, he found his own balloon pricked. The vice president in Kenya serves at the president's pleasure, and Moi decided that he was no longer pleased. In Parliament, Karanja, a Kikuyu, was accused of arrogance, disloyalty, corruption, and treason. He was forced to resign his position, drummed out of the party, and stripped of his passport.

So it was with Charles Njonjo, once one of the most powerful men in the country. Njonjo was one of those Kenyans who had been educated in England prior to independence, and joined the government after his return. A Kikuyu, he served Kenyatta as attorney general and became one of the president's trusted advisers. When Kenyatta died, Njonjo was part of the Kikuyu clique that gave Moi the support he needed to consolidate his own power. Eager for even greater authority, Njonjo ran successfully for Parliament and then joined the cabinet as minister of constitutional affairs. In that capacity, he made sure that the repressive colonial laws remained on the books and he used them in 1982 to suppress opposition in the move to a one-party state. But then Moi decided that Njonjo had become too powerful. Almost overnight, Njonjo found himself charged as a "traitor" plotting with a foreign nation to overthrow his own country. Condemned as a "betrayer" by an official commission of inquiry, he resigned from Parliament and went into political seclusion. Moi then cut off further discussion by taking the high road and quoting the Bible: "Let him among you who is without sin cast the first stone." When I visited Njonjo once at his large estate in Muthaiga, he seemed sober and subdued, comfortable with his much quieter life, but unwilling to talk about the carefully orchestrated attack more than a decade before that had brought him down.

Foreign Minister Robert Ouku, a member of the Luo group, was less fortunate than Njonjo. An attractive, articulate spokesman for national interests, he was highly regarded in foreign diplomatic circles and made the mistake of drawing attention away from Moi on an official visit abroad. He was totally loyal to the president, but he made the government uncomfortable because some people spoke of him as a possible successor to Moi. Others feared that he might expose vested interests in a campaign against corruption. In February 1990, his badly burned body, with a bullet in his brain, was found near his home in western Kenya. Luos were outraged at what appeared to be another political killing. When an official commission pointed to the involvement of Nicholas Biwott, a Kalenjin like Moi and the president's closest adviser, Moi dismissed Biwott and later ordered his arrest. But Biwott survived that scandal, as he had others, and was soon back in the cabinet.

The president had still other weapons in the arsenal he used against those considered to be political enemies. Imprisonment was one. Most detainees were held without the filing of formal charges. Attorney John Khaminwa, now a lead member of the commission investigating the Goldenberg scandal, spent a year in detention in the early 1980s after taking the case of a top police official who had been reassigned to a less influential position. When I visited him in his cluttered office in downtown Nairobi, he reflected grimly on the tiny cell in which he spent twenty-two hours a day alone, taking care of all human needs in that minuscule space. It can break people, he observed, but it failed to break him. A decade later, as agitation over the Ouku murder helped spark political opposition, the president clamped down even further on the dissidents. Kenneth Matiba, a leader of one of the opposition parties, was incarcerated. While in captivity, he suffered a stroke, which many Kenyans believe was induced by the torture he endured. Following a year of treatment, he returned to politics, but without the same incisiveness he had shown in the past.

At the same time, the administration undermined freedom of the press. Newspapers and magazines of various political persuasions appeared on the streets, but, until the late 1990s, operated under tight constraints. In the early part of the decade, for example, the government decided it was uncomfortable with the criticisms of *Finance* magazine and the *Nairobi Law Monthly*. Agents of the administration invaded the firm that was doing the printing for both publications and smashed the printing presses beyond repair. The message was a chilling one for both the publications that were silenced and for others watching the attack.

Toward the end of Moi's presidency, the governing party—KANU— owned one newspaper and had a financial interest in another. The *Nation* remained independent, but still faced constant pressure. Managing Editor Tom Mshindi, a thoughtful exponent of press freedom, spoke to me in 1997 about the difficulties of trying to preserve a measure of press freedom in a repressive state. "When you get a call from State House, sometimes you get a call from the president himself, and you are summoned to go and talk to him, that kind of works on you," he observed wryly, as he acknowledged that he had himself been twice summoned in the past few years. "The meeting was not one of an intimidating nature," he recalled of one encounter. "It was trying to work on my sensibility as a Kenyan, to try to help me understand why these things should be done differently." It was sometimes hard to ignore such pressure, he noted, especially when you knew what the consequences might be.

Conditions had improved in the past few years, Mshindi acknowledged, and the modest liberalization was the direct result of increasing public pressure for reform. The first step came on July 7, 1990, when activists held an unlicensed public meeting in Nairobi to call for multiparty democracy and more general political reform. The police moved with characteristic brutality and twenty-nine citizens died in the attack. Hundreds more were injured, and more than a thousand were arrested. "*Saba Saba*"—Kiswahili for "seven seven" (reflecting the day and the month)—became a rallying cry in the quest for a more liberal state. Two years later, more than a hundred thousand dissidents gathered at the Kamukunji fairgrounds, where the *Saba Saba* attack had taken place, to continue their campaign for reform.

External pressure also contributed to the drive for multiparty democracy. American Ambassador to Kenya Smith Hempstone, an abrasive but effective advocate for reform, led the effort. He secured an American commitment to press for reform, and persuaded other donor nations to join the campaign. In late 1991, ten donor nations, along with the World Bank and the International Monetary Fund, froze about a third of the $1 billion earmarked as aid for Kenya. Almost immediately, Moi capitulated and ordered the constitutional change that permitted other parties to function openly at long last.

Elections were held in 1992, with a number of different parties competing. But the government resisted issuing national identity cards, necessary to vote, to between 3 and 4 million young people who had come of age since the last campaign. Meanwhile, Parliament quietly passed a law mandating that, in order to win the presidency, a successful candidate had to gain at least 25 percent of the vote in five out of the country's eight provinces. Given the regional focus of the various opposition parties, that measure virtually ensured that Moi was the only candidate who could achieve a successful result. Though he received far less than a majority of the total votes cast, to no one's surprise, he retained the presidency.

But the reformers refused to go away. Several years later, a number of them banded together to try to unify the opposition. They formed a new organization, called *Safina*, or "Noah's Ark," in Kiswahili. In the forefront of this campaign was Richard Leakey, the noted paleontologist, who now dedicated all his energy to political reform.

Leakey had gained political visibility as head of the Kenya Wildlife Service, where he had almost single-handedly cut back on the ruthless acquisition of ivory by poachers who were wiping out Kenya's elephant population. "Shoot to kill," he had told his rangers, and they did. In the process, Leakey made powerful enemies who stood to lose financially from his actions and, although he had presidential support, it soon evaporated and he lost his job. Later, as Moi began to fear Leakey's growing popularity among Kenyans, he lost his tenure as head of the Kenya National Museums as well. Meanwhile, a plane he was piloting developed engine trouble in what virtually all Kenyans I spoke with considered an act of sabotage, and, in a terrible crash, Leakey lost both of his legs.

Harassment of political opponents continued. When I arrived in Kenya to teach in the summer of 1995, newspapers carried the story of a savage attack on Leakey and a number of other reformers. They had gone to Nakuru, a large city about two hours north of Nairobi, to protest the trial of one of their colleagues on trumped-up murder charges and to visit him in jail. Government-sponsored thugs tore them from their vehicles, beat them with chains and tire irons, and prevented them from gaining access to the jail or the prisoner they had come to see. Newspaper photographs showed the slashes on their backs and other parts of their bodies.

Yet Leakey remained optimistic, vital, and committed to reform. I spoke to him in the summer of 1996, then went back to see him the next year. I came away with the hope that, perhaps, Kenya might manage to get through hard times after all. In our first conversation, he declared, "There are changes in the pipeline." *Safina* was not yet registered, as required by the government, for Moi and his associates were determined to keep the reformers in limbo until the government could win still another election. A year later, *Safina* still remained unregistered, yet Leakey noted that "there's no such thing as never in this game, and whether Moi registers us is not the issue. We *will* be registered eventually." Registration came just before the 1997 election, too late to make a difference

Working behind the scenes, Leakey and his colleagues managed to keep the issue of reform in the forefront in the late 1990s and first years of the twenty-first century. At the same time, other reformers continued the campaign in the streets. Students, pressing for lower fees and more substantive political reforms, were already on the rampage as I arrived in Nairobi in the summer of 1997. I was tear-gassed as I worked my way past one confrontation between students and police and headed toward my hotel. All attention was riveted on the forthcoming *Saba Saba* day rallies commemorating the first protest demonstrations seven years before. Leakey spoke to me about the demonstrations that lay ahead: "The likelihood is that one or more of them will get out of hand. People may be killed, sadly. I don't want people to be killed, but I think they almost have to be killed for this thing to actually work."

When I asked about the personal price of this effort, Leakey smiled wryly and answered, "At the moment, deep frustration. Financial hardship, very considerable. I guess part of it is things like legs." And yet he continued, in part, he told me laughingly, because of the "missionary gene" in his family.

Leakey proved prophetic. In Nairobi, in 1997, university students (some I had taught a year before) continued to press for change. In an echo of the flag-burning protests in the United States in the Vietnam era, a number of them set a Kenyan flag on fire just outside the elegant Serena Hotel. Police broke up that gathering, as they smashed the main rally, on the grounds that it had not been legally registered. But the police did not stop there. They also invaded the All Saints Cathedral, the main Anglican church in the city, and the country, and brutally beat reform leader Reverend Timothy Njoya and other allies who were praying in the sanctuary. At the end of the day, ten people were dead nationwide. The following day, another four died.

CNN and the other major networks carried footage of the carnage in the United States and elsewhere in the world. In Kenya, censorship kept such images from the screen. One independent television station showed a brief clip of the invasion of the church, and government pressure led to the prompt dismissal of those in charge. Newspapers carried pictures of the violence, but in the rural areas outside Nairobi where literacy is less extensive, local inhabitants had a much more circumscribed picture of the chaos that had occurred.

In the aftermath of that upheaval, the country, and the world, watched and waited to see what would happen next. An election was required by law in the next several months. No one doubted that Moi would win, as indeed he did, though with a reduced parliamentary majority. But the president was getting older, and was not going to live forever. In some ways, as Leakey observed, the next election, and not this one, was really the crucial one. Constitutional reform was most important of all. As he observed, "We do feel that without constitutional reform, there is really no point in getting rid of Moi."

Change finally came in 2002. Moi was forced to step down after a fixed number of terms as specified in a constitution he could not change. Opposition groups came together in what was called NARC—the National Rainbow Coalition—and nominated Mwai Kibaki, a longtime politician and former vice president who enjoyed considerable respect, to stand against Moi's hand-picked successor, Uhuru Kenyatta, a young and politically inexperienced son of the first president. Kibaki won an overwhelming victory, was sworn in as president a few days after the election, and ushered in a new era. When I returned to Kenya in the summer of 2003, to lead another foreign-study program for American students with Sara, there was a stronger sense of hope and possibility than I had ever seen before.

Can Kenyan corruption ever be contained? Can the Parliament, for all of its imperial formality, ever become a truly democratic body able to exercise its authority effectively? Most people hope so. Some wonder, however, if full-scale reform is really possible. *Kitu kidogo*, the Kenyan way of conducting any business, is so deeply ingrained that it would take a monumental effort to root it out. Yet that effort is finally imaginable as talks unfold about drafting a new constitution, and the new president continues to do his best to promote national and not personal interests. Kenyans do want change. Those both in the provinces and in the cities feel that their own livelihood will only be enhanced by a regime committed to providing the services they need without skimming off so much of the funding in the process. But that kind of transformation will require a strong commitment if it is to bring about meaningful change.

Time and Tradition

The meeting was scheduled for 2:00 P.M. at the American Cultural Center in Nairobi. I arrived a few minutes early and found no one there at all. Impatiently, I sat down in a corner near the shelves holding current magazines and began to leaf through those that had arrived since I was there last. Half an hour later, the first of my Kenyan colleagues appeared. Half an hour after that, a few more friends straggled in, and after casual conversation that lasted another fifteen minutes, the meeting began.

This pattern occurred over and over during my stay in Kenya. It frustrated me at first, until slowly I came to terms with an altogether different conception of time. Punctuality is hardly considered a virtue in Kenya, or, for that matter, in most parts of Africa. As one friend explained to me, it was still two o'clock until the clock struck three o'clock and, by that reckoning, a meeting was hardly late if it started within that span. Given such flexibility, what did it really matter if it began even later, especially if no one kept track? The meeting, he said, would start whenever all the participants had arrived, and there was no use worrying about trying to begin any earlier than that.

I knew all this in my mind, of course. I had confronted similar patterns at other points in my travels. But I still struggled with what I considered tardiness for much of my stay abroad, despite strenuous efforts to make myself define lateness in different terms. Even when I *knew* others would show up well after the agreed-upon time, I couldn't help myself from persisting in arriving when I thought I should, as if to preserve my own sense of American identity or retain what I felt was a necessary control over the patterns of my own life. My major concession to Africa in this regard was learning not to get irritated or upset when I then had to wait, sometimes for hours, for a function to begin. Over the course of the time I spent in Kenya, I like to think I became at least marginally more flexible and began to accept patterns governing the use of time that even I had to admit came to make more sense to me. In the process, I think I slowly came to understand something of how the Kenyans themselves interpreted time — and the even more important link between time and tradition in African life.

Being on time was a virtue as I grew up. For most of my life, I showed up for classes, and appointments, and meetings as promptly as I could. As a child, I was often in a hurry to move from one thing to the next. I was raised with a sense of responsibility, and so wanted to do what was essential, when it needed to be done, and then move on to the next thing, whatever it might be. At the same time, my mother always counseled me that for social functions it was polite to be late. Just a little bit late. Better to come to a dinner party five or ten minutes after the specified time, she said, rather than at the moment indicated in the invitation. And heaven help you if you arrived any sooner than the time indicated by your hosts. A few minutes, it seemed, were important.

My two years in the Peace Corps, in the Philippines, exposed me to an altogether different conception of time. My Filipino friends were fond of joking about Filipino time, which meant arriving anywhere an hour or more after the time an event was scheduled to start. (Anywhere, that was, except at St. Peter's College, the institution run by German Benedictine nuns where I worked.) Filipino time entailed arriving late. American time meant arriving at the specified time. German time meant arriving early. Over the course of the two years I spent in the Philippines, I made my peace with these different patterns of telling time. I learned when I needed to show up to meet with other people and became adept at arriving at the appropriate time.

Many years later, after my divorce, as I shuttled children back and forth from my house to my former wife's house, and still tried to teach my classes, chair my department, and write my essays and books, I found myself pulled in all directions. Despite a deep-rooted and now-revived commitment to being on time, as I drove more than 30,000 miles a year, I found myself running late for virtually everything except the classes and meetings where promptness was non-negotiable. My parents and children joked about my deteriorating punctuality, though I was doing the best I could.

As my children, Jenny and David, grew up and went off to college, life became simpler. I found it easier to get to meetings and appointments on time, and to finish things I had started when I said they would be done. And then I met Sara and began to visit Africa and found myself remembering the more relaxed patterns I had known in the Philippines years before.

How much I learned not just to adapt, but to enjoy, the different conceptions of time was brought home to me on one of my return trips to Kenya. I had been pushing hard at home to complete all kinds of tasks and assignments on time before I left the United States. As I got off the plane in Nairobi, I was exhausted after traveling for about forty-two straight hours. Approaching the battered old Mercedes my taxi-driver friend Justus drove, I saw he was having a problem opening the door on the driver's side. The lock, which I remembered had given him problems in the past, simply wouldn't work. The lock on the passenger side was broken, too. We couldn't get into the car. In the United States, I would have called AAA for assistance, but that wasn't possible here. Instead, Justus forced the door and window just a bit, to be able to insert a piece of wire. Other people gathered around, until there were nine people involved in the operation, all offering advice. I let myself relax and felt the fatigue disappear, as I accepted the fact that I was back in Kenya and recognized that there was nothing I could do. About half an hour later, they were successful in opening the door.

Not everything in Kenya began late. Meetings at the American Embassy or dinners at the ambassador's residence all started on time. But at these functions, Americans were usually in charge, and invited guests or officials appeared when they were expected. Much to my surprise, classes at the University of Nairobi likewise operated with the punctuality that I expected back home. The university bureaucracy proceeded with a glacial slowness that never failed to frustrate me, but classes started and ended on time. Students, who took a heavy load and had more contact hours than their American counterparts, still managed to move from one classroom to the next promptly and efficiently. I could plan to begin a class at the stroke of the hour, and knew I had to end it at the appropriate time, so that students could move on to their next commitment. A few students wandered in late from time to time, but no more so than I was used to in the United States. Because I knew another instructor was waiting to use my classroom whenever I vacated it, my own punctuality was likewise important. On one occasion, the professor preceding me went longer than the specified time, as my fifty students and I waited in the hallway. When my students (not I) got restless and finally persuaded me to knock on the door, to signal that it was time for him to leave, he surprised me by apologizing for his tardiness.

Up-country, rural Kenyans who work on small farms seldom wear watches or rely on clocks. They rise with the sun and return from work when it sets, tilling the fields for as long as they can, and then relaxing at home, according to the rhythms of sun and moon and rain. Time is subsumed by the larger forces that affect their lives. While people in Nairobi operate in more bureaucratic and professional ways, and many now have cell phones and all of the office machines and communication devices that have become a part of Western life, some still rely on more informal means to orchestrate their sense of time.

Those patterns, however, can cause problems when transferred to the United States. When my student Jeremiah arrived in the Midwest to begin work on his M.A. degree at Miami University, Sara and I invited him over for dinner one evening. We asked him to come to our house at 6:00 P.M. An hour and a half later, I called him on the phone to ask where he was. He was still at home, with a watch on his wrist, but he had not bothered to look at it, since it had not begun to get dark yet. Nairobi is located close to the equator, and the sun rises and sets at about the same time—close to 6 A.M. and 6 P.M.—every day. Jeremiah had no sense of the seasonal difference in the length of the days, or the curious pattern caused by daylight savings time in the United States. He was waiting until daylight began to fade before coming over to our house.

As I walked across Nairobi with my friend Irungu one day, to a meeting we both knew would start late, he helped me understand better the Kenyan conception of time. Irungu had not yet traveled to the United States, though he was about to embark on his first trip there to begin study for a Ph.D. Despite his lack of first-hand experience, he was like many Kenyans in his passionate curiosity about America and American ways, and how they compared to Kenyan patterns. Contrasts to America come easily to many Africans, and people in other countries, inundated by the images and artifacts of American popular culture now available throughout the world. From what he knew, Iringu told me, Americans, rushed *through* time, and were always in a hurry, without ever pausing to look around. Rather than enjoy time, they sought to use it for their own ends. It was a commodity to be broken up and divided into smaller segments to provide the means for accomplishing specific tasks. Efficiency, which often entailed juggling a variety of different chores, meant working effectively within this framework. Time was less a part of daily life than a form of currency that could be spent in the on-going effort to get ahead.

When Americans met one another on the street, Irungu said, they greeted one another expansively, but in a kind of shortcut code. "How are you?" an American might say to a friend or colleague, or even to a stranger just met, without really expecting, or wanting, a full response. Indeed, an American might well be taken aback if the person greeted launched into a full-blown account of the problems faced just then. After a quick interchange, most Americans were ready to move on.

Africans were different, Irungu observed. Time was a *part* of daily life. If you met someone on the street, it was your obligation to stop and talk, for however long that might take. *Habari yako* is the standard Kiswahili greeting all over Kenya. Literally translated, it means "Your news?" and is usually followed by a standard response: *Nzuri,* which means, quite simply, "Good." But, unlike in America, this quick conversation is just a prelude to a more extended discussion that can sometimes last for hours and allow parties to ascertain the well-being and whereabouts of numerous relatives and friends. Never mind if others are waiting for you or for a meeting to start. It is more important to let conversation unfold according to its own rhythm.

As I watched my friends and neighbors, it seemed to me that Kenyans of all social classes spent lengthy periods of time with one another, talking, joking, drinking tea or coffee or beer together, in sessions that often extended throughout the day and sometimes went into the night. At the university, there were always groups of people in the Senior Common Room engaged in animated conversation. Friends who went out for beer and *nyama choma* (roast meat) stayed together for hours. People regularly came by our neighbor Mary's flat and visited for a while, invariably eating and drinking something before they left. Up-country, visits always took time. It was impossible to drop in on someone for just a moment. Inevitably, tea had to be served (and occasionally a chicken killed and cooked and eaten) before we were free to leave.

I spent much of my time in Kenya watching how Kenyans spent their time. As I walked across Uhuru Park in the center of the city on my way to work, I always saw large numbers of people loitering, lingering, even sleeping on the grass. This was not just a weekend or holiday phenomenon. The pattern of moving slowly, or sometimes not moving at all, held true any day of the week. Tourist T-shirts worn by white visitors in Nairobi proclaimed *Hakuna Matata* (No Problem), the now-classic slogan popularized in *The Lion King*, or the less poetic, more pointed variant in English alone, "No Hurry in Africa." A *mzungu* from America might laugh at the slow pace encountered in Kenya and move into a more relaxed holiday mode. For Kenyans themselves, this pattern was a way of life.

The idleness I saw was hardly laziness. Life was not easy for anyone in Kenya, save for members of the upper class with money to spare, and even the tasks I took for granted at home, such as buying groceries or other supplies, required far more effort in the part of Africa I came to know. Going to the open market, bargaining for vegetables with first one, then another vendor, and finally walking home or finding a *matatu*—a minibus—to provide transportation took substantial energy and consumed a good part of the day. Coping with the notoriously inefficient local or national bureaucracy likewise took inordinate amounts of time. Even at those rare times when the administrative apparatus worked smoothly, things moved slowly at best. All the more reason to relax whenever you could.

Time was also a commodity that did not need to be parceled out. Unlike most essentials in Africa, it was never in short supply. People might have to scrounge for food, or deal with shortages of teaching materials or other items we consider necessary in our lives, but time was always available to them. It was an asset to be savored and enjoyed, and most of my friends made the most of it whenever they could.

As the year wore on, I came to realize that the Kenyan sense of time was likewise related to a powerful sense of tradition. Time was a continuum that extended back for decades, even centuries, and helped frame the customs followed today. Tradition served as a kind of social cement and ethnic-group obligations held the nation together, providing a source of stability on a continent overwhelmed by the forces of change. Such obligations created a link with parents, grandparents, and other family members, and with the still-pertinent patterns of the precolonial past. Over the course of many generations, Kenyans have viewed their elders and ancestors with deep respect and followed carefully prescribed patterns for dealing with life and death. This had become clear as I watched the mourning ritual for our philosopher friend Odera, after he had been killed by a truck. It was equally clear in other circumstances as well.

As I learned more about the force of tradition in Kenyan life, I heard repeated mention of a celebrated court case in Nairobi a decade before. I vaguely remembered hearing about the case at the time, for it was followed by newspapers around the world. But now the patterns it reflected made more sense.

The case began in 1986, when S. M. Otieno, a distinguished Kenyan attorney suffering from hypertension, died of a heart attack. He was a Luo, who had married a Kikuyu and rejected many of the customs with which he had been raised. Despite the grumbling of family members, he had followed his own bent for most of his life. But now deep-rooted customs came back to haunt him in death, particularly as his Luo relatives demanded that their traditions be followed, regardless of what he or his wife preferred.

Otieno had discarded his Luo heritage. He had refused to teach the Luo language to his children or to share Luo customs with them. Before he died, he told his wife Wambui that he wanted to be buried on his farm in Nairobi, in the shadow of the Ngong hills, rather than be taken up-country, as Luo tradition demanded, to the land of his birth.

His wishes carried little weight with Luo family members, particularly since he had neglected to file a formal will. His brother and other relatives claimed that they owned the body and that neither his own wishes nor those of his wife and children had any bearing. It was essential to bury the lawyer on his ancestral farm, or his angry spirit would wreak untold havoc on his family. The Luos believed that accidents, infestations, and other evil occurrences all stemmed from the actions of an irate ghost from the past whose body had not been properly laid to rest.

Wambui had little love for the Luos, in general, or for her Luo in-laws, in particular. Indeed, animosity between the Luos and Kikuyus extends back for centuries and is reflected in the struggles among groups that continue to plague Kenya today. The Kikuyus, with about 5,000,000 members in a country of 22,000,000, are the most numerous, and, at least until President Daniel arap Moi consolidated his position, the most powerful. The Luos, numbering about 3,000,000, are the second largest, and jealous of Kikuyu privileges and prerogatives. The Kikuyu practice circumcision of men and, at least in the past, of women as well; the Luo do not. The Luo up-country remove lower front teeth; the Kikuyu do not. Each group has a damning stereotypical assessment of the other. As correspondent Blaine Harden observes in his book *Africa: Dispatches from a Fragile Continent*, "The Luo see the Kikuyu as denatured, money-hungry business people aping Western values as they betray their African heritage. The Kikuyu see the Luo as histrionic devotees of primitive traditions, with stout hearts, good singing voices, and soft heads."

Wambui was determined to challenge the prevailing Luo customs. One concern was keeping Otieno's estate intact. She knew that, when a wealthy Luo died, relatives often descended on his home and helped themselves to his possessions, which they now considered their own. To avert such a calamity, she rolled up the carpet and removed all appliances and other valuables that could be moved. She told the morgue not to allow anyone to view the body without her explicit written permission. At the same time, she went ahead and had a grave dug in Nairobi, while the Luos countered by digging a grave in Nyalgunga, Otieno's childhood home 200 miles away. Both sides filed court injunctions to prevent the other from moving the body until the case was resolved.

Wambui and her attorney, John Khaminwa, were well aware that they faced an uphill battle. As he later told me, "I knew from experience burial cases tend to be extremely sensitive, emotional, partly because of certain philosophical reasons that the African community tends to have toward death." But neither Wambui nor Khaminwa anticipated just how notorious the case would become.

The first court that heard the case ruled in favor of Wambui. The judge, a white British attorney working for the Kenyan government as a High Court judge, declared that he saw no reasons that traditional customs should bind someone eager to embrace Western ways. Otieno, he said, "was a metropolitan and a cosmopolitan, and though he undoubtedly honored his ancestors, it is hard to envisage such a person as subject to African customary law and in particular to the customs of a rural community."

Almost immediately, a three-judge Court of Appeal took up the case. Told that Otieno's body had already been embalmed and was in no danger of decomposing, this court issued an injunction restraining Wambui from burying the body until a ruling on the appeal had been handed down. Three weeks later, the judges rebuked the British judge for his unwillingness to acknowledge the force of local custom and called for a full trial.

The trial itself became a public spectacle. When Wambui took the stand, she testified that Otieno "told me that there are some Luo rituals performed after the death of a husband to which he would not like us to be subjected, such as building a hut symbolizing his home, where I would have to sleep the whole night with his body and a *juneko* [lunatic in the Luo language] would be paid to allegedly remove demons. I would also have to wear my husband's clothes inside out and my hair and that of my children would have to be shaved. After his burial, elders in his family would sit down and nominate a man to be my husband. My late husband did not want either me or our children to be subjected to these rituals. I don't think I can go through that." The attorney cross-examining her called her a lying "Kikuyu lady" responsible for pulling her husband away from his ethnic roots. The Luos in the courtroom booed her.

The audience was further outraged when Otieno's son Jairus testified. Even more Westernized than his father, he was then a student at William Paterson State College in New Jersey. The Luos were upset when Jairus tried to discount his Luo heritage and affirm his Kenyan identity, and became angrier still when, under cross-examination, he demeaned his elders. In response to the question, "Are the people lazy?" he answered, "As my father said, they are lazy. I saw how they cultivated and even what they do and, yes, they are lazy people."

Luos argued that there was a necessary distinction between house and home. Otieno lived in a house in Nairobi, but that was just a hollow structure, for his real home was up-country, in the land of his birth, and nothing he had done in the course of his life could change that inalterable fact.

Expert witnesses completed the Luo case. Odera, our Luo philosopher friend, surprised many of his colleagues when he claimed in court that "If you do not comply with customs, you may not be successful in your work. Your children may die. Or whenever you buy livestock, they die, or you could sire a child without legs."

While President Moi made no explicit public comment about the case until after a decision was handed down, it was widely rumored that he supported the Luo position. Given government control of the judiciary, and its relentless effort to control all parts of Kenyan life, it was assumed that there was pressure to uphold the Luo stand.

In early 1987, the High Court ruled in favor of the Luo side. The Court of Appeal upheld the verdict. Finally, Otieno was buried in the Luo village that was his original home, with two Anglican bishops, both Luo, presiding and

Luo customs, including the stampeding of cattle to drive away evil spirits, prevailing after the churchmen had left. The government released local secondary-school students from school so that they could greet the winning lawyer and celebrate the "African customs" that had been vindicated in the case.

Tradition triumphed. The forces of change beckoned but had been turned back, at least for a while. As Justice S.E.O. Bosire declared in his ruling, "Times will come and are soon coming when circumstances will dictate that the Luo customs with regard to burial be abandoned. Change is inevitable, but . . . it must be gradual."

But not much had changed a decade later, when I saw another, though less public, indication of how strongly tradition still governed people's lives. The major difference was that, this time, the case involved a personal friend.

This episode occurred in Kaimosi, in Western Province. Sara's program for her American students in 1995 included a month-long component there, where the students lived with Kenyan families. The area is the home of the Luhya group, and is also a stronghold of the Quaker faith. As missionaries from a variety of different denominations moved into Kenya almost a century ago, the Quakers became the dominant religious force in this part of the country and grafted their religious patterns onto the traditional local framework.

Sometimes that arrangement caused friction, especially when religious demands conflicted with customs that extended far back into the past. I saw the bifurcation between these different patterns, for example, as I watched circumcision rites in the fall. The Luhya circumcise their young men, and all adolescents who come under the knife in a given year remain part of the same cohort in the community for the rest of their lives. Yet some families choose to go through Church-guided circumcision procedures, instead of joining those who elect to participate in traditional circumcision rites that entail their sons living with the other boys and their elders for a full month in the woods, as a way of learning ancient lore and coming of age together in a powerful shared experience. Each group complains about the rigidity of the customs of the other, and the conflicts between the two approaches continue to divide the region today.

The case in Kaimosi involved the family of Elijah, a dignified man in his early sixties, who worked as an *askari*—a guard—at the guest house that served as the headquarters for Sara's program. He had lived in Kaimosi all his life and, like most of his counterparts, he had no other visible means of support outside of his small family farm. What he earned from working every night for the month the Earlham College program was there, making sure no thieves broke into the guest house, supported him and his family for the rest of the year. A warm, friendly man with gray hair, a wide grin, and tattered clothes that never seemed to fit, he preferred speaking in the Luhya language, but could converse comfortably in Kiswahili and haltingly in English. He and David, his fellow *askari*, used to join us at the guest house for dinner each night in Kaimosi, and together we spoke in a combination of languages about the events of the day.

Occasionally, Elijah invited Sara and me to his home, about a mile from the guest house. We parked our car by the side of the main road and then hiked in, crossing a river by balancing on a narrow log that served as a once-makeshift and now-permanent bridge over the fast-flowing water. We walked past small fields of maize and through Elijah's tiny tea field, all the way to his house.

Like most Kenyans, Elijah lived in a small compound surrounded by the homes of his sons. Among Luhyas, daughters moved away when they got married; sons were expected to stay nearby, both before and after they took a wife. Elijah's own house was a modest structure, built out of mud and wood. The front door opened into the dirt-floored living room, which had a small table and a number of unpainted, wood-slatted chairs. From time to time, a chicken wandered into the room, only to be shooed out by one of the embarrassed family members. Posters of a white Jesus, with quotations from the gospel and commands to live a good life, covered the walls. Electricity had not yet come to this part of Kaimosi, but the sounds of a battery-powered radio filled the air.

Every time we came to visit, Elijah's entire family turned out to meet us. He had six sons and three daughters. Those who were there gathered around, eager to participate in an exciting and out-of-the-ordinary event. Assorted grandchildren were so numerous that we frequently had trouble keeping track of them all. Agnes, Elijah's wife, invariably greeted us warmly and insisted that we share a meal with the group. And so we sat, waiting for her to start the fire, cook the *ugali*—corn paste that is a staple of the Kenyan diet—and make the stew and chicken that were always served to guests.

In midwinter, after Sara's students had finished the semester and gone back to the United States, and we were living in Nairobi, we learned about a terrible tragedy in Kaimosi. Rogers and Joseph, two of Elijah's unmarried sons, had quarreled, and Rogers had picked up a board and hit Joseph with it. Joseph stumbled out the front door, fell down, and hit his head. Family members took him to the local hospital to get medical care. At first, there was no doctor available. When a physician finally arrived, he diagnosed Joseph as suffering from malaria, which had troubled him the day before. Because medicine was inevitably in short supply, aspirin was all he prescribed. When Joseph began to have headaches and slipped into a coma, the doctor suggested that he be transported to another hospital, where an X ray might be taken, but such arrangements, where no one owned a car, took time to make.

Meanwhile, Joseph began to make noises and disturb the other patients, and so the medical staff gave him an injection of sleeping medicine. With his transfer imminent, Joseph awoke, became lucid for a moment, said he wanted to leave, then died.

This was horrible enough, but Elijah still had to deal with complications surrounding the death. He took the required step of going to the subchief to report the death. Yet now he faced the most important decision of all. According to local custom, whenever one family member was responsible for the death of another, he or she was to be sent away forever, banished from the family for all time. But Rogers was only sixteen, still a student in school, hardly able to create a new life for himself on his own. Elijah viewed himself as a Christian, and his Quaker faith embraced the notion of love. He could not send Rogers away and compound the tragedy that had already torn his family apart. Instead, he quietly buried Joseph in the yard in front of his house and let Rogers continue to live at home.

Now other villagers, some of them jealous at Elijah's good fortune in working for Sara's program from time to time, reacted with anger. Elijah's act in ignoring local tradition threatened to disrupt the entire community. Evil spirits were likely to curse everyone, they said, unless something was done.

They went to the police and, a couple of weeks later, authorities came and arrested Elijah, his wife Agnes, and young Rogers. They were taken to Vihiga, a nearby community, where they were put in jail. Agnes was released after one week, Elijah after another week, when friends (Sara and me included) provided the necessary funds for what we thought was bail but might have been a bribe. Rogers remained in prison for the next nine months. I had heard stories about Kenyan jails, but was still unprepared for the grim scene I saw when we went to visit Rogers at the police station. There were two cells behind the main desk, one for men and one for women. Each included dozens of prisoners scattered around the room. The main door had a tiny window, but the glass was stained and discolored, and I had a hard time seeing exactly what was inside. Light was virtually nonexistent and toilet facilities were barely adequate. In Kenya, it is not uncommon for a person to be held for days, weeks, even months without formal charges being filed. It is also not uncommon for a person to die in prison before a case has been resolved.

Rogers was in sad shape when we saw him in the jail. He was gaunt, having lost about fifteen pounds before we arrived. Now, for a price, the family was permitted to bring him food every day, and he looked forward to the visits and the meals.

At long last, the case reached a judge. Weakened and overwhelmed, Rogers fainted during the hearing. Instead of reviving him and seeing if they could continue with the legal procedure, the police returned him to the cell, where his case was rescheduled for the next month. He still had no word whether he was going to be tried as a minor, where a measure of leniency was possible, or as an adult.

When Sara and I left Kenya in the summer of 1996, Rogers was still in jail, despite assurances extending back several months that he would be released sometime soon. Eventually, after still another few months, we learned in a letter that reached us in the United States, that he had been freed and allowed to get on with his life. The court had found him not guilty of killing his brother, preferring to believe that malaria was the real cause of death, but the court could not back down entirely and, in a face-saving gesture, put him on probation for the next three years.

Yet local custom still decreed that he had to be sent away. And so Rogers was now living with a relative of his father in a community about fifteen miles away, and would continue his education at a private boarding school in that community. Elijah had no money at all for such schooling, but Sara and I were able to help.

Everyone in Kaimosi, and even in other parts of Kenya, knew about the case. The *Nation* printed a story about the incident. Whenever I asked about the episode, people were quick to report what they had heard. Some members of the Quaker church recognized the difficulties the incarceration was causing the family and secretly believed that the village response to the crisis caused by Joseph's death was wrong. But traditions change slowly at best, and no one was willing to say publicly what a number of them felt privately. They accepted tradition as a necessary part of their existence, and would have been hard pressed to function without the structure and rhythm it created. While Jack, one of Elijah's older sons, wrote to us that "as Christians we know this is the work of the devil and through prayer he shall be overcome," others unrelated to the family were less sure.

Tradition, even when it led to tragedy, was vitally important to my Kenyan friends. It provided a link to the patterns of the past. It served as a buffer against the forces of change that intruded on the configurations they had found comfortable, or at least familiar, in years past. Kenyans needed to maintain their ties with their ancestors to retain a sense of harmony in their own lives. For most of them, it made no difference that more and more people had mobile phones or that computers were finally starting to gain a foothold in the country or that CNN appeared on television in wealthy homes. Kenyans, particularly those in the countryside, still defined the world in terms of their own traditions, and according to their related conception of time. Life moved slowly, and in traditional ways, regardless of modern intrusions. People were patient now, as they had been in colonial times, when faced by unwelcome but unavoidable demands of the British, and the pattern of moving slowly and deliberately in the face of provocation provided a necessary link to an earlier age. Kenya might be trying desperately to develop in Western ways as it looked to the future, but an unshakable sense of tradition often seemed to link it even more firmly to the past.

On the Road

My first priority after settling into our Nairobi home in 1995 was buying a car. Sara and I were going to be in Kenya for a full year, and I wanted to be able to explore the country at our own pace. You can go virtually anywhere in East Africa on public transportation, as we had in the past, but it can take hours, perhaps days, to get from one place to the next, even when a site seems nearby. I knew we would rely on buses and *matatus* from time to time, and we looked forward to taking the British-built train to the coast, but we still wanted to have the flexibility to move around at will. Besides, what self-respecting American could even imagine spending an extended spell anywhere without an automobile for personal use?

A car used to be a luxury in Kenya. In colonial days, and even in the first years after independence, only wealthy Kenyans could afford their own automobiles. But times have changed, as prices have dropped and cars have become more available, and people of modest means now purchase vehicles. Cars are still not cheap, especially given the painfully-low standard of living so prevalent in much of the country. Yet middle-class Kenyans, particularly those in the professional ranks, make whatever sacrifices are necessary to buy their own cars. Most of my university colleagues had automobiles, and I was relieved to find that I would not feel like an ostentatious foreigner if I bought one.

Today, the streets of Nairobi are clogged with more vehicles than the city can absorb. Some cars are European- or American-made, but most of the vehicles come from Japan, with Toyotas, Nissans, and Hondas most visible. In 1995, virtually all of them were white. A city street sometimes looked like a vast white wave as vehicles moved together or sat in a traffic jam. The common color sometimes caused confusion, and I occasionally walked out of a store or into a parking lot and tried to enter the wrong car.

Before I could drive anywhere, I had to figure out where to buy a car. One
friend suggested reading the advertisements in the newspaper. Another told
me to go out to the United Nations headquarters in Nairobi, where expatriates
on their way home often had automobiles for sale. Another suggested I read
the American Embassy newsletter, which likewise listed goods that departing
diplomats were trying to unload. Still another suggested that I make a quick
trip to Dubai, where I could find a reconditioned car at half the local price,
even, he claimed, adding in the expense of the journey abroad.

I thought about all of the alternatives. At first, making telephone calls was
difficult, for our phone didn't yet work. Then, when it was finally connected,
the intermittent service made it hard to reach anyone in Nairobi. The UN center was outside of town, relatively inaccessible without a car of my own. And
the embassy alternative likewise failed to work. The only car for sale at the
time was one that had been in a wreck, and the honest owner ruefully told me
that it still didn't run right, despite extensive repairs. I ruled out a trip to
Dubai. We had just arrived in Kenya, and I was hardly ready to leave.

Justus, our always-helpful taxi-driver friend, suggested that I try the West-
lands car bazaar. Every Sunday, he said, people gathered in a large field along
Uhuru Highway, right next to one of Nairobi's first large shopping centers, to
buy and sell cars. It was an informal, unregulated version of an East African vegetable market, only here people were peddling vehicles. This was my chance to
see a large number of cars at the same time. I jumped at the opportunity, especially when Justus said he would come along and help me look around.

There were hundreds of cars in the muddy field. People with automobiles
to sell arrived at dawn to stake out a good site, in the hope of being able to
sidetrack prospective buyers as they walked by. Some were selling luxury vehicles, like Land Rovers and Pajeros, which were far more expensive than I
could afford. Others were trying to sell cars that looked like contraptions in a
Saturday-morning cartoon. But there were also a fair number of ordinary automobiles that seemed as though they could serve my needs. I wanted one of
the older white cars I saw all around me, which, I assumed, might be within
my means.

I looked for an undented automobile. Justus listened to the engine of first
one car, then another, checked out the color of the exhaust, and suggested that
a car that had a couple of blemishes might be a better bet, for such a vehicle
would be less enticing to thieves. I took his advice and, after a couple of
hours, settled on a white Nissan Sunny, a four-door sedan, assembled in
Kenya in 1989, that seemed just what I had in mind. Best of all, Peter, the
owner, had been the sole driver of the car.

Now it was time to negotiate. As in a vegetable or craft market, no self-
respecting customer would pay full price. Bargaining is part of the whole

process, and must be done over an extended period of time unless you want to be taken for a total fool. Peter and I bantered back and forth for a few moments without settling anything, as Justus looked on in amusement. Finally, I wrote down Peter's full name and telephone number (wondering if the phone would really work) and went home. Later that afternoon, I called him and told him I wanted to go for a test drive and to have a couple of mechanics, both of them Justus's sons, take a look at the car.

Peter brought the Sunny around the next day. It drove smoothly, in the short spin I took around Nairobi (driving anxiously on the left side of the road). Much to my relief, Justus and his sons told me the car was in good shape.

I offered the Kenya shilling equivalent of $6,000, what Justus said the car was worth. Peter, as new at this process as I was, laughed nervously. He countered. I hedged, equally nervously, then came up a bit. Ten minutes later, we had a deal, and I was pleased. I was going to have to pay a little more than I had anticipated, but I thought I was getting a good car.

Buying a car was but the first step. Now I had to keep it running smoothly. The Kenyan roads were so rough that this was no easy task. Dodging potholes became a personal contest, and one I invariably lost, every time I got in the car. Some roads had eroded so badly that driving on dirt became a way of life. Under such circumstances, tires blew out frequently. I became adept at using the jack, but I found it was also almost impossible to keep the car aligned.

Fortunately, Justus's son Njoroge was a first-rate mechanic, who spent hours working on my car, and subcontracted the work to equally capable friends when he needed help. Through Njoroge, I learned about the *jua kali* approach at first hand. *Jua kali* means hot sun in Kiswahili, and is used to describe any kind of work done outside in the open air by artisans or their assistants, without the benefit of a well-equipped shop. Over the years, it has come to refer to an informal approach to making or repairing virtually anything.

With a working car in our hands, Sara and I took to the roads. We drove around Nairobi, spending hours in traffic jams in the congested streets. We dodged oncoming cars trying to pass slow trucks on the narrow two-lane road winding through the Rift Valley. Mindful of the road carnage that became the focus of a vivid newspaper campaign, we tried to be as careful as we could; looking at the buses and trucks overturned by the side of the road every time we ventured out persuaded us of the constant need for vigilance.

Still, I remained relatively undaunted and used the car to travel all over Kenya. Sara and I drove south to the coast and north to Lake Turkana, site of some of the great palaeontological discoveries of our time. When Sara's American students were in Kaimosi, in Western Province, I could drive up there to visit in half a day, just about half the time the bus took. When her group moved to Lake Naivasha, near the entrance to Hell's Gate National Park, I could make it from Nairobi in an hour and a half.

Getting directions, however, was sometimes a challenge. In a fit of optimism, I had bought the best maps available, only to find that they didn't always show all the roads. Although American men are supposed to be reluctant to ask directions, even when they are hopelessly lost, I found stopping a stranger to be a necessary, and even enjoyable, experience. Kenyans walking along the road were friendly, even to an American *mzungu*. They were usually amused at my halting attempts to use Kiswahili and eager to be helpful. I was grateful whenever a local inhabitant offered to get in the car to show me where I needed to go.

Sara and I traveled even more when we had visitors to show around. East Africa acts like a magnet, attracting tourists from around the world, and Kenya is a favorite destination. Once Sara got through with her semester-long program, we had a non-stop stream of visitors. And so we all piled into our car—or a rented vehicle, if warranted by the numbers—and headed off on safari.

First my children came over for a month. Then Sara's parents arrived. The next month, my sister and her son, along with two of their friends, came over. Two Miami University colleagues spent a day with us. Then two other Oxford, Ohio, friends, in whose home Sara and I had first met, arrived in Kenya, eager to see Africa for the first time. We decided to take them on a tour of our favorite spots, just before we left the country at the end of our year abroad.

Sara became a kind of amateur travel agent, poring over guidebooks, examining road maps, and plotting routes for us to take. With the same meticulous attention to detail that she used in planning her student program, she made the arrangements for all of our excursions. "Do you think we should stay at Loldia or Borana or both?" she would ask rhetorically as she began to outline a next trip. Early in our stay, we stumbled upon a small book entitled *Kenya's Best Hotels, Lodges & Homestays*, written by three women formerly associated with the American Embassy, and it became a key source in our explorations. Because we were in the country for an extended period of time, with Kenyan driver's licenses of our own, we were considered residents, and the rates we had to pay for lodging became much more affordable than what tourists were charged. Between the suggestions we found in that collection and the background stories provided in Richard Trillo's *Kenya: The Rough Guide*, we were ready to head off in any direction, confident that we would be comfortable wherever we went.

East Africa's mountains had a special attraction for me. Every time we headed north toward Nanyuki, we passed Mt. Kenya, looming large in the clouds. On my first trip to Kenya in 1990, Sara and I had trudged up this mountain, the country's highest peak, but had only made it to about 15,000 feet. The three-day trip was my first experience mountain climbing, and even though I had suffered altitude sickness, with a splitting headache and an upset stomach that only got better when I began to come down, I was ready to try again.

The following year, when I returned to Africa for a six-week trip, my children, Jenny and David, joined me in climbing Mt. Kilimanjaro, just across the border in Tanzania. At 19,340 feet, Africa's highest mountain seemed like the ultimate test. Over a five-day period, I did my best to heed our guide's instructions, as the Kiswahili words *pole, pole*—slowly, slowly—echoed like a never-ending refrain. This time I heard more about altitude sickness from other climbers going up and down. Before I had just considered it an unpleasant inconvenience. Now I began to realize that, in the worst case scenario, altitude sickness could cause pulmonary edema—where your lungs fill up with fluid—and even death.

On this climb, we all did relatively well for the first few days. Each night, after ascending another 5,000 or 6,000 feet, we rested comfortably in huts provided by the Tanzanian park authorities for climbers like us. On the third day, as we reached close to 15,000 feet and found ourselves crossing the saddle—a long stretch of trail where nothing at all grew and the terrain seemed like the desolate surface of the moon—Jenny gave out. She began to heave, and remained sick for the rest of the day. Soon she was stopping every ten feet, sustained by a helping hand, eager only to get to the next hut to lie down.

That evening was the toughest of all. Though she didn't have pulmonary edema, Jenny had difficulty keeping even fluids down. As we ate the same meal for the third successive night, David and I lost our appetite as well. We went to bed at 6:00 P.M., totally exhausted and short of breath, only to lie awake listening to other sick people in Kibo Hut leave at periodic intervals to go outside.

At midnight, Baraka, our main guide, came to get David and me, to take us to the summit, while our second guide promised to take Jenny down to a lower elevation in the morning. We walked with only the light of the stars and a flickering kerosene lantern. Up ahead, another group snaked toward the top of Africa, its lanterns making it look like an electric caterpillar as it inched forward. It was good that none of us had more light. If we had been able to see the steepness required for the final ascent, we would never have wanted to climb.

A thousand feet farther along, David stopped. "Come on, David," I cajoled him. "You can make it if you try." But David would have none of my urging and his dry heaving persuaded me that he needed to return to a lower level. Baraka and I turned around, ready to give up the attempt and take him back to the hut. Then, about fifteen minutes later, we came upon another group with a friendly guide, who told Baraka to take David down alone and agreed to take me to the top with his group.

Five hours later, as subfreezing winds whipped around the summit and dawn broke with a burst of pink light, we could sense we were close to our destination. "*Pole, pole,*" we told ourselves, though we had no choice. Three or four steps up, then pause for a minute to calm our stomachs and catch our breath. Finally, as the sky became bright, we made it to Gillman's Point, which the guides count as the top. We could have walked around the crater rim for another hour and a half to Uhuru Peak, just a little bit higher, but most members of the group were sick enough that none of us wanted to try. We stayed together, relieved just to be able to look around.

Descending was easy. The footing was tough from time to time, but each step took us to a lower altitude, where it was easier to breathe. When I found Jenny and David at Horombo Hut, at about 12,000 feet, both felt fine. We made it down the next day to our hotel at the base of the mountain, ready for a warm shower, a cold beer, and a dinner different from what we had been eating for the past five days.

Having conquered Kilimanjaro, I was ready for other mountains. The next year, I climbed Popocatépetl, just outside Mexico City, all the way to the top of the 17,887 foot peak. Using crampons and an ice axe, I felt like a semi-experienced climber on that trip. Now that I was back in Africa, I was eager to try Mt. Kenya again.

This time, the climbing party consisted of five people. Sara opted out, having had her fill of mountain climbing for her entire life. My sister Karen was worried about the effort ahead. Her friend Laurie was equally apprehensive about the altitude and was concerned about her knees. Mike and Garrett, the fourteen-year-olds in the group, had no such fears. My biggest concern was that they would plunge ahead too quickly, and either lose the trail or fall victim to altitude sickness, which can hit even those in the best of health. Fortunately, they were used to living in high places—in their part of Wyoming, the elevation is over 7,000 feet—and they were in good shape. And I knew that altitude would be less of a problem for me than before, after living at close to a mile high in Nairobi for more than half a year.

The five of us piled into the Nissan Sunny, and headed off for our point of departure—the Naro Moru River Lodge at the base of the mountain. There was good food, a pool, and a sauna, all situated among lush flowers, with the mountain looming overhead. We ate well and relaxed in preparation for the climb. This was going to be easy, Garrett said.

The next day, it began to drizzle in midafternoon as we were driving ten miles in a Land Rover that lacked springs to pick up our guide at the trail gate.

Then came a seven-mile uphill hike in the rain from the park entrance to the first overnight hut—Met Camp at 10,000 feet.

It was relatively easy thus far. Our guide served as our cook, and prepared a meat-and-vegetable stew that reappeared at each meal over the course of the next three days. Seven porters carried the sleeping bags and food for the five of us. As the air got thinner, we appreciated that assistance more and more.

The next morning, we took off on a six-hour hike all the way to Mackinder's Camp at 14,200 feet, as a relentless rain continued to fall. The route wound first through a rain forest, then up the appropriately-named "vertical bog," where we had to step between clumps of grass into pools of water while ascending, up further still to open land where the only plants were giant lobelias—large cabbage-like clumps with an occasional spike rising up toward the sky. Finally, we followed a ridge along a cliff for a while, before descending to our cold stone cabin that would be our home for the night.

There was a cloud cover as we settled into the cabin and tried to get warm. We could see nothing through the windows except sheets of rain. I tried to nap, but the altitude made it difficult to sleep. About all we could do was wander around the cabin and try to eat. Why was I doing this? I wondered to myself, but kept quiet to avoid discouraging the others.

In the evening, as dusk fell, the rain stopped and the clouds disappeared. Now we could see the mountain looming above us by the light of the moon. It was a striking scene, much like an Ansel Adams photograph in stark black and white. I reveled in the quiet calm as we nestled into our sleeping bags for the night. At the same time, I was concerned about the steepest part of the climb, which lay ahead. I could now see how steep the mountain was, and I knew the kind of effort it was going to take.

At 3:00 A.M., our guide roused us for the final ascent. Karen and Laurie decided that they had gone far enough and elected to stay behind. Mike, Garrett, and I headed off into the night. The rain had stopped, and the way was clear. A full moon made the top peaks of Batian and Nelian stand out like huge slabs of craggy rock in the starlit sky. Both peaks are just over 17,000 feet, but they are accessible only to trained, technical climbers. While I had been roped to my guide and had relied on my ice axe on my ascent of Popocatépetl, I lacked the expertise necessary for the Kenyan peaks. Our destination instead was Point Lenana, at 16,335 feet, which I had failed to reach on my initial attempt several years before.

The first part of the trail wound along a small stream, then began to ascend up the scree, the mixture of volcanic ash and ice crystals. Periodically, I muttered to the others, *"Pole, pole,"* in a frustrated effort to get them to slow down. *"Haraka, haraka, haina baraka,"* I continued, in an effort to signal to the guide that *I* needed to take it easier. This was a Kiswahili proverb which, loosely translated, meant "Haste brings no blessing." Reluctantly, the boys complied. Even so, we all reached Austrian hut, a small, unequipped shelter that looked like an outhouse in a frozen version of hell, in just two hours and had to sit shivering in the cold, waiting for a bit more light for the last ascent. "Damn!" I muttered to myself as I continued to shake.

I thought that Point Lenana was going to be easy. The altitude was not bothering me this time, and it was just another 600 feet up. But all the rain the past week had turned to snow on the top of the mountain, and what should have been a tough but satisfying scramble became an almost impossible climb up a sheet of ice.

Mike and Garrett scampered up, like a pair of mountain goats. Perhaps one of the benefits (and perils) of youth is that you feel no fear. I could admire their spunk at a distance, but had to admit I was scared. As I looked down, I could envision myself sliding down the peak, all the way into a nearby crevasse. I balked. "I can't go any farther," I said. Trying not to interpret this as a defeat, I refused to take another step.

My guide refused to listen to me. He climbed back down to where I was stranded, and then moved along, step-by-step, kicking holes for my feet in the crusty snow. Half an hour after the boys had reached the summit, I arrived. Bracing myself to avoid slipping off, I helped take photographs of us all.

Going down was easy. I could tell the boys were proud of what they had done. I was grateful for having accomplished what I had set out to do, even if it had taken a bit more anxiety and effort than I had anticipated. Picking up Karen and Laurie at Mackinder's Camp, we retraced our steps back through the "vertical bog," back to the park gate, back to our car.

With Karen and her group, as with Sara's students and later with other friends, we headed for Masai Mara, perhaps Kenya's best-known game park. Though it stretches for miles in all directions, it is just a small part of the much larger Serengetti expanse that extends across the Mara River and into Tanzania. The Mara includes all kinds of terrain—large savannah areas where millions of wildebeests graze in open plains following their migration from the south, wooded thickets where lions and sometimes leopards sleep during the day, rivers where dozens of hippos wallow in the water and crocodiles look like floating logs.

Getting to Masai Mara by road is part of the adventure. Twenty miles outside of Nairobi, the road begins to climb up the escarpment at the edge of the Great Rift Valley. The rift itself is a long geological formation running from north to south, where the earth's huge tectonic plates float on liquid magma far beneath the ground. The collision of these plates leads one side to rise up and form mountains—such as Mt. Longonot, a now-extinct volcano— looming in the distance, while the other side drops down. Most of these breaks occur beneath the surface of the ocean and cannot be seen. The one that forms the Rift Valley extends along the earth's surface for more than 5,400 miles, from the Jordan Valley all the way to the Zambesi delta. This long crack in the geological plate stretches around about a quarter of the earth's circumference. The sharpest definition comes in Kenya, and now we were driving across it from one side to the next.

As we drove across the Rift Valley, the heavily rutted road, poor even by Kenyan standards, sometimes made our visitors wonder whether the journey was worth the effort. Potholes often loomed so large that we spent most of our time driving along a dirt path along the side of the road. But the view was still spectacular, with the hills and mountains rising up on one side, and the larger, lower expanse of grassland on the other. Thorn trees, which often attract weaver birds with their wispy nests, were interspersed among stretches of bush grass on both sides of the road. Each time I went to Masai Mara, I was overwhelmed by the view and tried to persuade visitors that the rib-jarring ride was part of the adventure. They were invariably excited as we drew nearer to the game-reserve gate and began to see Maasai herdsmen, with their distinctive red blankets and bodies as tall and thin as their staffs.

Just getting past the gate can be an ordeal. As drivers park their vehicles to pay the requisite entrance fees, hordes of Maasai women, bedecked in the same colorful beads they are trying to sell, descend on the cars and vans. Most have close-cropped hair. Some have long stretched ear lobes, with the huge holes filled with oversized earrings. They thrust their beaded wares through open windows, with a few words of English indicating their asking price. They are willing to bargain, but know that the captive tourists have nowhere to go.

Inside the reserve, Masai Mara is filled with lodges and campsites, all booked in advance depending on what you are willing to spend and where you want to go. On occasion, Sara and I had stayed in simple tents, with Maasai *askaris*—guards—making sure that no elephants or other wild animals came too close to our site at night. At other times, we had headed for a more upscale location, a lodge, complete with a swimming pool and elegant dining room, or better yet, a luxury tented camp, where the canvas dwellings were as large as our bedroom back home and had indoor plumbing, double beds, and other amenities meant to put visitors like us at ease.

But the real attraction is not the overnight facilities but the game park itself. Here, as in Samburu to the north, or even Nairobi National Park, just a few miles from the center of the city, we drove, either in our own car, a rented vehicle, or a safari van, along the roads and trails that ran through the reserve. Often we departed on a first game drive at dawn, as some animals were just beginning to stir and nocturnal hunters were getting ready to go to sleep. On our first trip to Masai Mara, the migration of the wildebeests, moving from Tanzania into Kenya in search of better grazing, was in full swing, and we could see those who had made it across the Mara River. We watched these curious creatures, each with a heavy-set chest and horns following the line of their ears. Sometimes they arched their backs and bucked up and down in a playful prance. More often they simply grazed on the rich grass, oblivious to the vehicles. Interspersed were other animals, such as zebras so numerous that we began to take them for granted after a while. I learned to tell the difference between a Thompson's gazelle and a Grant's gazelle. I gazed at leopards one day and cheetahs the next. And, on one occasion, when our close friends from Ohio were along, we all watched a pride of seven or eight lions from a distance of about ten feet for the better part of an hour, as they lazed about in the summer sun.

Sometimes, the animals took us by surprise. On one trip, Sara and I were alone in our own car in Tsavo West National Park. We had spent the night in one of the two lodges, watching a leopard come out for bait as we sipped our evening drinks. The next morning, we explored other parts of the park before heading home. Rounding a corner, we came upon two herds of Cape buffalo, large, regal creatures, quite different from the buffalo that once roamed the American Great Plains. The Cape buffalo have horns winding down from the face and then circling back up as they return to the top of the head. These buffalo sometime look bored as they gaze listlessly at the visitors looking at them, but that look only masks a fierce temper in many of the males. At 1,200 pounds, we understood they should be treated with care.

I braked quickly and brought the car to a halt. The small Nissan Sunny seemed tiny in comparison to the eighty or more animals, with one herd on either side of the dirt road. I debated gunning the motor and trying to drive through, before they had time to react, then realized that it would have been a foolish move. A scene from *Jurassic Park* flashed through my mind, as I envisioned several of the huge creatures crumpling the car, as if it was a piece of tin trash to be thrown away. And so we stopped and watched them for the better part of an hour while they watched us. We were not in a hurry; we had no place in particular we needed to go. I felt like a naturalist in the bush, examining the every move of the animals. Eventually, they became bored with us, and slowly the two herds began to wander off. When they had cleared enough space on the road, I drove on at last, relieved that we could proceed without harm.

An even more nerve-wracking confrontation with animals came when Sara and I went for a one-night holiday to Lake Nakuru, the site of about a zillion pink flamingos. They have become world-famous, and can be seen on all the Kenyan tourist posters. From a distance, they appear to form a massive pink blanket, extending as far as the eye can see. As you move closer, the birds themselves become visible, but they are still almost indistinguishable. Only as you get closer still can you make out the individual birds, but even then you are still overwhelmed by the wonderful splash of pale pink color they make as the lake meets the sky.

On this particular trip, there were few birds to be seen. The lake had receded due to lack of rain, and most of the birds had flown off to other sites. The few flamingos left stood near the edge of the lake, separated from us by a huge salt flat.

As we drove closer, we could see tire tracks on the flat. Other cars before us had evidently gone near the water's edge. At one point, I began to have qualms as we got closer to the birds, but naively I drove on. Finally, I could see no other car tracks, and said to Sara, "I think we'd better turn back." I stopped the car, and as I threw it into reverse, I was suddenly afraid it might not move.

The car balked. It refused to go forward, or back. We were stuck.

Cavalierly, I told Sara to take the wheel while I pushed. The tires just sank deeper into the mud.

Off on the horizon, I could see the Lake Nakuru Lodge, where we had stayed the night before. It was about five miles away, with a number of wild animals between us and it. We had passed four rhinos, five Cape buffalo, and a host of smaller creatures in the last fifteen minutes. Now we had the choice of waiting in the noonday equatorial sun to see if anyone drove our way before nightfall or taking our chances and walking back to the lodge to get help. We decided—foolishly, I suppose—to walk.

And so we tiptoed past the buffalo, trying to avoid surprising them. I was wearing a red shirt, and I wondered if they would react to the bright color like angry bulls in a Pamplona ring. As we approached the rhinos, fortunately downwind, we ducked behind a small rise along the side of the road, hoping to keep them from seeing us. We didn't even let ourselves *think* about the lions and leopards that were probably roaming somewhere in the park.

Much to our relief, we made it to the main park road. And just as we reached the road, a truck from the lodge roared by. It braked quickly as the driver saw us, for people are not supposed to walk in the park. As we explained our plight in a combination of Kiswahili and English, the driver and his companion motioned us to get into the truck. They would take us back to the car and help us get it out.

Relieved, I learned a new Kiswahili word: *mjinga*—foolish (or perhaps even stupid). They said it over and over, and I knew full well they were talking about me.

As we approached the salt flat, we left the truck and walked the rest of the way toward the lake. The two Kenyans and I tried to push the car, while Sara gunned the motor. It still refused to budge.

Just then, another vehicle came into view in the distance. Though we were half a mile away, we were able to flag it down. Two men and two women, all of them British, came our way.

With eight people pushing, we managed to move the car just a bit. But each time we got it to shift a little, it seemed to sink even deeper into the mud.

Finally, one of the British men suggested taking everything movable out of the vehicle. Then we removed the rubber mats from the floor and laid them next to the wheels. With all of us straining, we managed to lift the car onto the four mats and then to push it gently toward more solid ground. We did not stop pushing for a couple hundred yards.

Only as we put all the muddy objects back in the car and drove off did the whole experience begin to sink in. We were out of trouble. Soon we were out of the park. We had weathered the breakdown. Our car was moving again. I felt lucky to be alive, a little *mjinga* to be sure, but back on the road.

Many of our excursions, both with and without visitors, took us to the coast. Indian Ocean resorts attract tourists from around the world, eager for an African holiday that includes time in the sun. Mombasa is a favorite destination. It is Kenya's main port, and the busy and bustling city includes market stalls, spice shops, and open-fronted stores along Biashara Street, where tourists and residents can buy the *kangas* and other pieces of colorful cloth that many rural Kenyan women wear. Souvenir stores with soapstone sculptures and wooden animals are ubiquitous as proprietors hawk their wares, often following tourists down the street to assure them of a good price. Fort Jesus, built by the Portuguese in the late sixteenth century, still stands, a classic European structure with giant walls meant to keep all intruders away. But Mombasa is hot and humid, whatever the season, and most tourists come to relax at the seaside hotels.

On the beach, they are on are safari—only without the animals. They eat, drink, swim, and cavort in the sun, much as they would on the Riviera or in the Canary Islands, in an attempt to enjoy as much as they can of the good life before returning home. The large hotels—the Nyali Beach Hotel, the Serena, and a host of others—cater to the tourists' every whim. Beach boys wander along the shore, looking for women who have come for a wild fling. Men can find similar amusements in more discreet ways.

While we enjoyed Mombasa and the amenities it offered when we needed to relax, we went more often to Lamu, a small island a couple hundred miles up the coast.

Here I found myself far away from the hustle of the high-powered tourist life. The tiny town of Lamu, accessible only by sea or by air, has but one land vehicle—a jeep used by the chief administrative officer. The Islamic tradition prevails, and many of the women still wear the *buibui*—the long one-piece

black gown that Swahili women wear in public, leaving little of the body visible. The Kiswahili spoken is the purest in all of Kenya, and has a lilt different from what I was accustomed to hearing in Nairobi. Liquor is proscribed,
and for the most part unavailable, though a few establishments have found
ways to serve it to their guests.

People have lived on Lamu for hundreds of years, though the special Ara-
bic flavor is of more recent origin. The Portuguese first came in 1505, and ex-
tracted a cash tribute from the local king. Toward the end of the century, the
Turks threatened, then were driven back. The Portuguese were finally de-
feated by the end of the seventeenth century, as nomads from nearby areas invaded the region. The Arab influence, which came first from traders in past
centuries, became far more important in the nineteenth century, as Omani sul-
tans established their dominance in the region, and gave the city, and island,
the character still visible today.

There are mosques everywhere on Lamu. First built by Arab traders for
their prayers, one dates back to 1511, while another contains a sacred stone
from 1370. Most, however, were built in the last two hundred years. The
mosques are an essential part of the life of the town. Wherever I stayed, I
could hear the haunting, minor-key call to prayer well before dawn and at regular intervals punctuating the day.

The town of Lamu itself fronts on the ocean, with a large sea wall running
the length of the town. Many of the buildings facing the sea have pillars. Behind them winds a maze of narrow streets, with stone houses all featuring
shuttered windows and ornate carved timber doors. Inside, the houses usually
contain a courtyard, where family members gather. Outside, by the front door,
stone benches still provide a place for the head of the household to meet his
male friends. Open sewers carry water, not all of it clean, from higher points
down toward the sea.

The city has several thousand donkeys that vie with people on foot in the
narrow passageways. An English-based charity provides a sanctuary for old
and lame donkeys. Young men ride the animals recklessly down the streets as
if they were fast cars. Donkey droppings appear everywhere and, after a few
squishy steps, I learned to watch carefully where I walked.

Many of the hotels in town are situated in the old stone houses. Few of
these have air conditioning, and most are cooled only by ceiling fans that
cease working when the electricity goes off. Lamu is often hot, especially in
December and January. Yet the town has a charm as it moves at an old-world
pace, closing down at noon for an extended break, and it always made me feel
as though I was staying in a special and unique place.

I wandered for hours up and down the narrow streets, looking in at small
shops where proprietors were as willing to talk as to sell their wares. I loved

walking up the island to the beautiful white sand beach, with the sea on one side and midsized dunes on the other. There were some other tourists, especially at peak season in the summer, but it was always possible to walk further and find a place of your own. Often Sara and I took visitors out for a *dhow* ride on one of the local boats, each with a single sail, that dot the harbor at all times. Sometimes our guide tried to help us catch fish, laughing good-naturedly as I failed to hook anything at all. The guide was invariably more successful, and then took us to another island to build a fire and cook our lunch on the beach. At sunset, I loved feeling the quiet breeze over the water, as evening crowded out the day.

One *safari* took us in the opposite direction—all the way up to Lake Turkana in the desolate north. The lake itself, also known as the Jade Sea, extends along the floor of the Rift Valley in the midst of thousands of square miles of dusty plains and volcanic rock. Shaped like a long, thin, beckoning finger, it stretches all the way up to the Ethiopian border. Along the east side, about two-thirds of the way up, lies Koobi Fora, a large paleontological site that became famous twenty-five years ago when Bernard Ng'eneo, a Kenyan assistant on one of Richard Leakey's expeditions, found a fragment of a skull that pushed back the date of human evolution about half a million years. Other equally exciting discoveries followed in later years, as Meave Leakey replaced her husband as the chief paleontologist in the family.

Turkana is remote and not easily accessible. In the midst of Sara's semester-long program in 1995, her American students had a week off and could go wherever they chose as long as they returned to Nairobi on time. Several venturesome students decided to take intermittent public transportation and then hitchhike the rest of the way to the eastern edge of the lake when they reached the point where there was no other way to get further. They made it to South Hor, a tiny rural outpost with virtually no link to the world outside, in a couple of days, then found they were stuck. Three days later, they begged a ride with the first vehicle that appeared, a truck heading south, and rejoined the group late.

After the students departed, Sara and I took our trusty Nissan Sunny up the somewhat easier western route. We headed through Eldoret, a reasonably-sized city near the homestead of President Moi, then continued on to Kitale, a much smaller city near Mt. Elgon, along the route to Uganda. From there, a fully paved, well-maintained tarmac road stretching about 300 kilometers took us all the way to Lodwar, a hot, dusty town in the middle of nowhere, about an hour from the lake. Some years ago, a Norwegian development team had built a fish processing plant there, and had constructed the road to provide the needed access. But the power requirements proved too great, and the experiment came to an end. In search of lodging, we found a primitive conference center, likewise started by a development project, and stayed there, the only guests in this barren place. The next day, we drove into town to buy gas and ask directions to the lake. The attendant insisted we take a young boy, perhaps twelve or thirteen years old, along with us. He needed to get some school papers signed near the lake, the man said, and he could show us the way. With his help, we headed north for another hour, past the non-functioning fish processing plant, along a sandy path that reminded me of our ill-fated approach to Lake Nakuru, and finally stumbled upon Lake Turkana itself. After wading in the water and wandering along the shore, we were ready to leave. There was nothing to do, nowhere to go, and no way to escape the intense heat. We got in our car and returned to Lodwar, then Kitale.

But we knew that the east side of the lake was more imposing. Mindful of the experience of Sara's students, we understood this was hardly a trip we could make in our Sunny on our own. And so we signed up for an eight-day safari with the Gametrackers company and headed north with fifteen travelers in a large, converted truck. Each of us carried a sleeping bag and enough water for the entire trip.

The first day was easy, on roads, first tarmac then dirt, all the way to Samburu National Park. I was delighted to make this stretch of the trip again, with someone else behind the wheel. A friend had dropped an axle on this road, and I had been afraid we might do the same thing on a previous trip. It was much easier in our industrial-size truck. Then we continued further north, to Marsabit, either a large town or a small city, depending on your perspective, and on to North Hor. As we reached the desert, the road disappeared. Most of the time we drove across a parched landscape, with only an occasional solitary tree and long stretches of volcanic rock to break the monotony. Once, we stopped near a dry river bed, picked up some loose firewood, drove the truck over it to break the wood into pieces, and bound it to the back of the vehicle with rope so that we could make a fire later that night. On another occasion, the truck got stuck in sandy terrain, and so we all piled out, put planks under the wheels, and pushed it forward. As I realized that we sometimes spent an entire day without seeing another vehicle, I was relieved to know that the driver had a radio that kept him in contact with Nairobi, even though we broke the antenna as we brushed against a tree. After crossing the Chalbi Desert, we ended up at Loiyangalani, a hot, dusty oasis on the shore of the lake.

We stayed in a camp Gametrackers had built a few years before. It was dotted with small huts, built out of sticks and straw, much like the homes of the Turkana people of the region. An open space that served as the door looked out at the sea. Though the sun was brutally hot in the cloudless sky, a constant breeze cooled us off. The safari company provided meals and an endless supply of beer.

Crocodiles live in the lake, and, we were told, would welcome a human meal. But the safari company had created a swimming area at the end of a rocky path by stretching chicken wire under water from one point to another. It hardly seemed stable, and I imagined a hungry crocodile could chomp through it in one gulp, but after a first cooling dip, I put my doubts aside and spent hours in the sea. When the water got cold, the sun and wind dried me off in a matter of moments. More than anywhere else in Kenya, I really felt off the beaten track.

Later, we went off in a boat to visit the Elmolo people, Kenya's smallest ethnic group, further north on the shore of the lake. Life is even harder here than in other parts of the country. Nothing grows in the volcanic terrain, and fishing means facing the crocodiles in unstable boats. The beads and trinkets we bought provided the sole source of income for many of the families in this barren place.

The trip to Turkana highlighted the contrasts between different parts of the country. This *was* a uniquely beautiful region, a stark and stunning wasteland where life unfolded with an elemental simplicity in the midst of spectacular geological formations. Even as I wondered how people lived in this area, I took a special delight in sitting quietly with huge piles of volcanic ash all around, watching the sun drop quickly over the horizon above the sea. The lake has long had a mystical appeal for the people of the region. On this side, I could almost imagine the earliest humans wandering along the shore.

At the same time, this trip, and the others Sara and I took, underscored the contrasts between us and the people for whom Kenya was home. Cars may have been common in Nairobi, but only for members of the middle and upper classes. In the rural countryside, virtually no one had personal transportation. For them, trips entailed riding the buses and *matatus* and spending endless hours getting from one place to the next. Visiting a relative in the hospital could easily become an all-day affair. Shopping anywhere usually meant a long walk or a crowded ride in a public vehicle. The trips I made this way made me all the more grateful for the ability I had to move around on my own. On one occasion, I was heading toward Maasailand to join up with Sara's students who were camping in the Loita Hills. The road was so bad I was advised not to bring my own car. And so I rode a minivan for about four hours to Narok, where I then waited another two hours for a truck bound for Narosura to fill up. The driver and a couple of special passengers rode in the cab. Along with fifteen other passengers, some chickens, and a baby goat, I found myself crammed in the back, where there was enough bench space for about ten of us. On the dirt road, the dust roiled up and swirled back into the flat bed of the covered truck. By the end of the three-hour trip, I was filthy, grateful only to have been far enough from the goat to have been spared one further indignity when it relieved itself on the floor.

The car also gave me the latitude to do what I like to do best—travel on my own and explore new places. Our friend Mary, who lived next door, wondered why we were setting off all the time. "Don't you like it here?" she asked us, though she knew how fond we were of both the apartment and our neighbors and friends. Watching us move our bags into the car for another weekend trip became a kind of standing joke, highlighting the difference between her life and ours. She walked to and from the university. Every couple of weeks she took a bus or *matatu* to her family home in Meru. On occasion, she had made other excursions, but they were rare. She was a typical Kenyan, whose patterns were dramatically different from our own.

Mary was happy to see us enjoy her country, and to join us in our car for one wonderful trip to her rural home. We, meanwhile, reveled in the flexibility we had to go anywhere we wanted. I loved being able to go to places I had heard about, whenever Sara and I wanted to get off on our own. Kenya's extraordinary landscapes were there for us to explore, and explore them we did, in our typical American way.

Epilogue

After my first trip to Kenya in 1990, I returned again and again. Sara and I came back virtually every year, sometimes leading a safari, sometimes bringing students for varying periods of time, sometimes traveling alone. The more we came back, the more it felt like home.

Unfortunately, not all of our friends were there to greet us. Frank and Kip, two of Sara's favorite Kiswahili teachers, both died of the effects of hypertension. Robert and Mary, our elderly English friends, died within the space of several years. Mary had gone to Canada to attend her grandson's wedding and, after the long plane trip home, developed circulatory problems that eventually caused her death. Robert, who was unable to make that trip, finally died of old age after reaching ninety-nine.

Mary, our Kenyan neighbor and friend, was gone for another reason. She survived her divorce and, with Joy and Sheila, her two daughters, left for the United States in 1997 to pursue her Ph.D. I had heard about the African Studies Program at Michigan State University, and I repeatedly contacted one of the faculty members there, explaining why, although Mary's credentials might differ from the ordinary applicant's, she would make a strong contribution to the department. Finally, he agreed to bring her over, and authorized the fellowship support that was essential for her to enroll.

Fortunately, other friends remained. Gloria, who still serves as Sara's surrogate mother in Kenya, grew ever stiffer and hard of hearing. But we made a point of seeing her regularly whenever we came back. Justus, our taxi driver friend, continued to drive us wherever we wanted to go in Nairobi, to provide commentary about both Kenyan and American politics, and to offer us his herbal elixir for whatever emotional or physical ailments we had. Over the years, we began to see Godfrey, my colleague at the University of Nairobi, and his wife Margaret more and more. I had enjoyed periodic contacts with

147

them during the year I taught at the University of Nairobi, but in subsequent years we became far closer and now consider them real friends. They came to stay at our home during a visit to the United States, and later took us to their up-country retirement home in Nyeri, several hours from Nairobi. And Godfrey became the key contact in bringing Kenyan students to Miami University and other institutions in the United States.

Miami soon had a small community of Kenyans studying at the university. Jeremiah came first, received his Master's degree, then got a Ph.D. at the University of Wisconsin, and is just about ready to return to Africa. Once he had finished his Master's degree, the Miami History Department accepted another Kenyan, again with full fellowship support, then still another after he was done, creating a pipeline for capable students who just needed the chance. Other departments have proven equally hospitable. And Mary's daughter Sheila has just started as an undergraduate at Miami, with one of the institution's prize scholarships.

Sara and I began to travel to other parts of Africa—to Uganda and Ethiopia in the east, to Ghana, Côte d'Ivoire, and Mali in the west, to Morocco and Tunisia in the north, and to South Africa as well. As I write in the fall of 2003, we are leading another group of twenty Earlham College students on a program that is taking place in Tanzania, because a United States travel warning made coming to Kenya a problem. Our trips throughout the continent have opened up more perspectives to us, showing us just how much more there is to see. But they have also underscored our desire to return to Kenya whenever we can.

Frustrations still remain, to be sure, but those seem less bothersome. Cell phones make it possible to reach people more easily, and they also provide more convenient Internet access than land lines. The roads remain awful, somehow always worse than I remember, but people hold out the hope that they will be repaired soon. Patience, I tell myself.

For Kenya has just undergone the first peaceful transition from one political party to another, something the United States first experienced two centuries ago. And now the new government of Mwai Kibaki is seeking to root out corruption, rebuild the infrastructure, and restore faith in government. In 2003, there is a greater sense of hope and goodwill than I have ever seen in the past. No one expects the task to be easy. No one expects major changes to come overnight. But there is a commitment to writing a new constitution, reconstructing the country, and reclaiming Kenya's legacy of possibility, so strong in the first days of independence forty years ago. The nation is embarking on an uncertain safari, but one that most people believe will bring about a better country in the end. As for me, what began as my own uncertain safari in 1990 has turned into a powerful attachment to a part of the world I once knew almost nothing about but now consider a second home.

About the Author

Allan M. Winkler is Distinguished Professor of History at Miami University in Ohio. He has also taught at Yale University and the University of Oregon and, for one year each, at the University of Helsinki in Finland, the University of Amsterdam in The Netherlands, and the University of Nairobi in Kenya. A prize-winning teacher, he is author of eight books of his own, which include *The Politics of Propaganda: The Office of War Information, 1942–1945*; *Home Front U.S.A.: America during World War II*; and *Life Under a Cloud: American Anxiety about the Atom*, and co-author of the college textbook *The American People: Creating a Nation and a Society* and the high school textbook *America: Pathways to the Present*.